When Something Changes Everything

a companion and guide for recovering from loss and change

PETER McGUGAN

Potentials Press

D1440210

Potentials Press
2340 South Ridge Dr. Palm Springs, California 92264
Web Page: http://www.petermcgugan.com
Published in 1998 by Potentials Press
Copyright © 1997 by Peter McGugan
All rights reserved.

LIBRARY OF CONGRESS CATALOGING-IN-PUBLICATION DATA
McGugan, Peter
When Something Changes Everything / Peter McGugan

p.   cm.
Includes index
ISBN 0-9694312-1-X (soft cover)
1. Self Help   2. Psychology

cover design: Peter McGugan & Kauffman Graphics,
cover art: Will Klemm   interior design: Emily Cullen Nash
author cover photo (eyes): Romance Portraits, Los Angeles
Printed in the United State of America

THIS BOOK IS DEDICATED TO
SHATTERED HEARTS,
LOST AND ALONE
IN THE WHIRLWINDS OF CHANGE.
—P.M^cG.

Contents

CONTENTS

CONTENTS

CONTENTS

Reader Path: Accidents And Disasters

When Something Changes Everything

Reader Path: Career Change, Loss Of A Job

Peter McGugan

Reader Path: Death Of A Spouse

When Something Changes Everything

Reader Path: Loss Of A Child

When Something Changes Everything

Peter McGugan

Reader Path: Loss Of A Parent

When Something Changes Everything

Peter McGugan

Reader Path: Management

Reader Path: Separation, Divorce, Loss Of A Love

Peter McGugan

Surrendering

Beginning to Begin

Chapter One

This book is a companion and guide through the deep, dark valleys of loss. It translates the language of the heart.

It's for times when the peaceful sanctuary of sleep will not admit you and at four a.m. your consciousness buzzes, for those times when people you know and love don't know what to say or how to be with you, for those times you don't know how to be with yourself.

Loss and grief are our culture's last taboos, still unfit for public discussion. We've created a cacophony of pop culture diversions to distract us from the truths of life and death. The truth is, everyone and everything we have in our lives we release. And the skills of Change Masters are worthy lessons.

Loss is a common note in our rhythms of attracting, having and holding and then letting go.

We lose through death, sickness and departures; by growing; graduating; moving on. People, position and times we love slip away as we journey further from the youthful illusions and fantasies of sweet innocence.

Disillusioned, we learn to climb out of the deep valleys of loss and earn the vantage of wisdom.

The locomotive of change spares no one; as we age and lose resiliency, it stops at our doorstep more often.

Loss is so very devastating to us because we are the innocent generations. We are the first pupils of School-

➡

house Earth to grow up oblivious to the hunt and the kill, to daily death and to the fragile precipice of living. We are the first generations to not grow up witnessing the death that leads to our dinner, the life and death cycles of nature, the deaths of the warriors, the elders, and the effects of the plagues.

For us, these are only occasional news items preceded by soap operas, followed by game shows—until an impact hits home, your own home, and you find yourself adrift in a moment-to-moment emotional hell that doesn't resolve itself in Hollywood, microwave or fiber-optic time.

When something changes everything, the hollow ache can't be kissed away, worked away, drugged away or healed with a cookie or a shiny new car. We can't cut to a commercial and come back all better.

This is the real-time journey through the winter of the soul. It's what North America's pop culture seduces us away from all our lives until something real is gone.

And with devastating bluntness we learn: Life is a solitary experience in a group setting.

Change is the breath of life.

Change rules.

Resistance is the seed of pain.

Exhausted from clutching to what already slipped away, we must surrender and embark on this lonely odyssey of recovery and reinvention.

We must indulge strange internally driven emotions with honest expression as we go about the messy business of emptying ourselves of a precious former life.

We must begin to begin.

Peter McGugan

The journey's destination is a place of wisdom and joy, living with ease and grace. Our stops along the way are confusion, rage, exhaustion and despair.

You've already embarked; you're already in a different place.

Sometimes the path of recovery is narrow and jagged, too narrow for a companion. Friends don't know what to do or say.

There may be more casualties as aftershocks radiate through your life, sparing only the most solid elements. What survives is real.

Lingering where you need to, your schedule follows an inner path of baby steps and, occasionally, a leap. You must befriend, love, forgive and parent this strange new self. You are not your old self, you are your grieving self.

This is not something we've wanted to be good at. We've not been prepared or taught that this journey offers landscapes of rich, succulent loving and learning.

Feeling better with it, feeling further along, we suddenly get ambushed by the past. Again, we crumble and wail the sounds of the wounded soul.

For we, who view life through flickers on a screen, this internal wild-minded confusion, this whirring intensity, is excruciating.

Love burns hot as it sputters.

➡

When Something Changes Everything

My Story?

It was three deaths in one month—wretched, senseless, unfathomable and tragic endings to young lives that changed everything for me. The details of my gory losses are no longer important to me or you.

Birth and death are always bloody messes. Enough said.

My life recovering from loss I share openly. The who, what, where, why and how of my losses are my private past, not to be shared in books, speeches or on talk shows. How I've healed is what is of value.

In grief support groups I've seen people, six years after impact, still obsessed with the gory details of the event. Addicted to pity, they are junkies transfusing their bloody, tragic story into all who will listen.

For a time the telling of it is the healing. But when the story is dramatized as a pity evoking party piece, you are using it, not recovering from it.

When you begin embellishing to make it listenable again for others who are tired of it, it is time to give your gory story its funeral.

There Is No Right Way, No Timetable

There is no right or wrong way. There is no official timetable your recovery should follow. But there are common experiences, events and perceptions that I've gathered.

Together, let's venture on the tender paths of emotion and ego and journey the winter of the soul, anticipating a place and time we will not resent sunshine and laughter.

Peter McGugan

Your Guide

Your attention span is shortened, so I'm offering thoughts in bite-sized pieces.

This is a reference book, a companion and guide to covet and curse. It is alphabetized so you can identify a feeling and quickly find insights.

The reader paths are your road map through this book. Refer to them at the front of the book or use the tear-out pages at the back. Find the path closest to your loss.

When your reading gets ahead of your self, you'll feel pressured and angry with me. It's too much too soon.

Read and reread thoughts that match where you are.

The most frightening, difficult step in changing is the next one—the monster that stares and dares us to move through it.

Not moving gives fear its power.

If you awake each day and ask yourself *what am I afraid of today* and then approach that with research and wisdom, you will be healed and empowered.

Recovery must happen at your own pace; as long as you are taking baby steps into the future, you will gain the lessons, insight and life skills this experience offers. They probably aren't skills you've wanted, but they are your Ph.D. in life.

SEE: **ZERO ZONE**

Accidents

The impact of an accident can radiate through family, friends and community. Physical shock accompanies emotional and mental detonation. The dust settles and we feel fragile, stunned and numb.

The stages of grief—denial, blaming, anger—follow accidents. We grieve the illusions of invincibility and clearly see that every moment is armed with potentials for destruction or creation.

The hours and days following an accident are a whirlwind of soul pummeling nightmares.

Allow yourself to also grieve the loss of innocence.

As you are feeling something, try to name it and then read and reread that section of this and other books. Talk about the feelings you are having.

Seek out survivors of similar events. Discover how they've used an accident to blossom into a new chapter of their life.

With each loss there is a path to gains, gifts we would not otherwise have had.

If you scorn the gifts, your loss compounds.

SEE: **READER PATH: ACCIDENTS AND DISASTERS, ANGER, HOW GREAT PEOPLE HANDLE LOSS, FRIENDS**

Aka Threads

Ancient Peruvian tribes believed once you have known another's soul, you have an aka thread that links you eternally.

You've had the experience of thinking of someone you haven't seen in ages and encountering them the next day or of thinking of a friend and they call you.

We tug on aka threads.

No matter the Cosmic distance, threads of consciousness link us. We each weave threads into the tapestry that is Cosmos.

How is your panel in the Cosmic Tapestry?

Is it rich, colorful, beautiful?

Peter McGugan

Aloneness

To Love someone enough to let them leave, to Love enough to be peacefully alone, is to blossom with divine Love and higher faith.

By filling emptiness with your own presence, you win your Self.

Being alone is not what we fear. It is what we may do with that aloneness that is feared. What we fear is our own potentials.

The most constructive moments of any life are the private ones when, alone with Creation, we decide to surrender to this new truth, to choose love over fear, to believe a new dream, and to go for it.

It is not our pain that we fear, it is our own light.

Being alone with loss bestows a gentle, radiant beauty.

When a dark cloud descends, we ask, "Who am I to shine." I ask, who are you not to shine!

Who are you, in a world starved for so much, to turn away from your potentials?

SEE: **SOLITUDE, SUPPORT SYSTEMS**

IF YOU CAN THINK OF BEGINNING,
DO!
IF YOU THINK YOU CAN'T,
DO IT ANYWAY.

Peter McGugan

Anger

Anger is fear twisted inside out. Express the anger positively and then parent what's left of the fear.

To stay angry at Life without expressing it is to silently rage at totality.

Totality is too vast for loving souls, like us, to take on.

As a loving and wise parent, would you want a child to suppress frustration and never question why?

We learn by struggling, getting angry and letting our feelings out.

If you are angry at Creation, at guardian angels that looked away, then heal your relationship by releasing your feelings.

Have a heart-to-heart talk with God so you don't hold onto rage and carry a grudge.

In every relationship clearing the air is the biggest step toward healing.

➡

Anger: Ten Ways To Express It

- Transfer your feelings to the mattress by pounding it with a tennis racket, a pillow, a bat or a mop.

- Go somewhere remote and shout, scream and rage.

- Express your feelings through drawing, painting or writing letters.

- Go to a golf or batting range and focus your anger on the balls.

- Join a support group.

- Talk to a therapist or a therapeutic friend.

- Write epitaphs, ballads or poetry.

- Do an aerobics workout.

- When you need touch, have a deep professional massage.

- Ride a stationary bicycle or use a Stair Master machine.

Anger is a thing. Imposed on other people, it stays in our world. Surrendered to the Light, it is gone from here. Light penetrates all darkness.

SEE: **VIOLENCE AND REVENGE**

Peter McGugan

Approaches For Friends And Family

THE PROBLEM IS, THE FUTURE KEEPS ARRIVING
BEFORE WE'RE FINISHED WITH THE PAST.

Each person has an individual relationship with the
past...and the future. We must make peace with both.
Adaptability, patience and compassion are your most
valuable skills when parenting friends and family.

The following are ideas to share and teach by example.

Aim Your Attitude

Change makes us angry and afraid.

We become angry because our illusion of being in
control slips away.

Change takes the past and leaves us to learn and
reinvent ourselves without the previous plans or hopes.
And what we fear most are our own potentials to learn
the lessons and own the responsibility of reinventing
ourselves.

Anger, frustration, fear and disappointment are
normal and valid. Vent anger in ways that don't make
matters worse; then calmly apply your wisest voice for
the expression of your fears.

Ask the questions that trouble you. Invest in the
recovery plan.

➡

When Something Changes Everything

Change happens! And whatever you think about expands. So rather than concentrate on what's going wrong, become a change agent and throw your energy into solutions.

Within each change is opportunity; and the people with the positive, helpful attitude win life's prizes.

Seize this opportunity to shine from under a cloud.

Avoid Blame

How does holding a grudge work for you? While you are contaminated by anger and fear, who wins?

Criticizing, blaming and finger pointing don't change history or fix anything, so what is the point of using the present trying to redo the past?

You can't go back and reown the past, but you do own your future. Focus on that, because planning works better than blaming.

De-stress Before Distress

Adjusting to the new reality is work. It forces you to learn.

The emotional sorting out is exhausting and time consuming. If you don't make personal time for feelings, illness and burnout are a risk.

Take vitamins, get sleep and manage your stress load. Exercise and diet are critical during dramatic change. Relaxation tapes can help you unload fears.

Nurture yourself with loving self-parenting. Others may not have any to spare right now.

Peter McGugan

Change Squeezes Us

Old emotions get dislodged by change. Fear, guilt, anger flood out irrationally.

Anticipate illogical behavior and be caring, comforting and non judgmental as people purge emotional sludge.

Prepare To Parent

People will come to you for listening not managing. They need acknowledgment and agreement that what's happening is difficult...for everyone.

Become An Analyst

Before complaining, blaming or griping look for breakthroughs. Rather than just dumping a problem into the lap of your advisors think of three ways to fix it, talk the ideas over and manage the solution.

By using your expertise you'll be creating win/win solutions and safeguarding the future because you are managing NOW—the only time you can really influence.

Avoid No-Win Battles

When the winds of change blow through your life you have the choice of battling them or riding them.

With the wind at your back you can ride it, but you must take a forward looking stand to catch its lift and see its direction.

➡

NO ONE KNOWS ENOUGH TO BE A PESSIMIST.

Laugh

Life is a wild and crazy ride.
Get the absurdity.

When Strengths Are Weaknesses

Consistency and loyalty are usually strengths. But the usual is increasingly unusual in our world of accelerating change.

To thrive, you must learn to adapt.

Situations determine priorities and when something changes everything, adaptability is the skill that gets people through.

Shun Sabotage

What you put out into the world you receive back. Therefore what you try to destroy will try to destroy you.

Peter McGugan

Grow A Future

Nature adapts to change instantly.

Tornados strip the land in a moment, and as the dust settles the landscape has adjusted. The impact has passed and is already history. Seeds have been strewn and the regrowth has begun.

Nature surrenders itself to itself, but human minds and hearts are not so naturally adaptable. To recover gracefully, give up hope of having a perfect past.

The best way to create a safer future is to be a wise gardener and partner, preparing for the next season.

THE WISE PERSON BEFRIENDS THE ENEMIES
THEY MOST FEAR.

Asking For Help

Everyone is into their own personal agenda. Often we're too busy to see where our energy is needed most.

Being with a person who needs us is the best personal investment anyone can make.

There is no shame in needing help, no shame in asking. Most of us think we should only have to hint about needing help and when people don't respond, we go into pity-party-nobody-loves-me mode.

Asking once is not enough. We must ask three times when the person is listening.

Do not assume people know how bad things are. Tell them and you become a teacher, an instrument of opportunity for someone to do good.

There is a great difference between doing well and doing good. In our material quest to be perceived as doing well, we forget what counts. Doing good boosts the quality of life.

"I need to see you tonight...so drop by and bring dinner" is something I had to learn to say.

It felt awkward but better than the abandonment, loneliness and anger. And people appreciated me calling on them for help. They were pleased to help me in an hour of need and it brought us permanently closer.

Peter McGugan

Balance And Imbalance
Compulsions And Addictions

I mbalances are created when we rely too heavily on any one option, and we are most at risk of personal imbalance after something changes everything.

Our culture enthusiastically encourages us to numb our self, to suppress the day's feelings so we'll fit within the socially acceptable narrow range of moods, topics and awarenesses.

Cognitive psychologists tell us we have 63,000 thoughts a day. Unfortunately 50,000 are the same ones we had yesterday!

Feelings and thoughts are meant to flow so fresh ones can arrive.

Drugs create emotional and mental log jams.

Thoughts and feelings are the flow of your soul. They are real and legitimate things. Block their exit routes and they burrow deep, fester and then wait for expression.

During the most difficult events, drugs prescribed by a physician (who is aware of all the medications you're on) can help you get through the toughest times. But, to really get through this, you need to face the new reality in a sober state.

The popular misconception is that chemicals eliminate emotions. They don't; chemicals just put a temporary lid on feelings.

➡

Grief can be preserved for years, but it doesn't age well. It mutates and surfaces as rage, phobias, nastiness, workaholism, addictions, eating disorders, failed relationships, depressions and illness.

Ideas For Balance

- Make a list of your support systems. Include the music you like, pets, people, activities, healthy outlets for rage, healing places, things you'd love to try. Reference this list when you have needy moments and ask your inner wisdom what you really hunger for. Often it is a hug, a massage, forgiveness from yourself, a change of scenery. Develop skills for choosing from your support system.

- We learn to walk by stumbling and falling. Forgive yourself for learning this lesson. The paths in and out of destruction offer Life's most valuable lessons. Consider this your Ph.D. in Life.

- Get an album and set up wonderful purposeful goals for yourself. Write your wishes, clip pictures of the dream and keep moving toward it. Be careful what you ask for because you'll create it.

- Most importantly, find people who understand and know the path. Observe a support group like Overeaters Anonymous, Gamblers Anonymous, Sex and Love Addicts Anonymous, Workaholics Anonymous, Debtors Anonymous...

Peter McGugan

Look for these groups in the resource guide at the end of this book or in the white pages of your phone book. Any of these programs will refer you to the best one for you. Although it takes time to find your recovery group, it promises a sweet reward.

SEE: IMBALANCE, CHEMICAL DEPENDENCY, RESOURCE GUIDE

Be The Gift

Do you hide your gifts by choosing to be a self-pitying victim?

Endings are completions that invite beginnings and reinventions and these gifts can emerge from the void of loss.

This book did.

In your void, invite your special gift to emerge and find expression through you.

Be the gift.

Peter McGugan

Beginning To Begin

Enjoy yourself. And if you can't enjoy yourself, enjoy someone else!

There are wondrous situations, activities and people being positioned for you. Nature abhors a void, but you can maintain a void with your silent rage. You can strain against the delivery of happiness.

Your past is behind you—what you do now is fight your future. Each time you choose anger over forgiveness, fear over love, you sabotage what life is preparing for you.

Angels cry and your loss compounds.

Are you ready to change?

You say you're sick and tired of being sick and tired? This section is for people at the intersection of who you are and who you want to be.

Here is your guide for blossoming into your new season of living. It's tough love in places. It involves cleaning house and moving toward a new dream, but the rewards are the sweetest life can offer you and all who love you.

Embrace A Healthy New Culture

The old culture is designed to protect itself, not bring about its own end.

When the circumstances, players and climate of that old culture have already changed, you must free yourself through actions in stark contrast to past procedures.

➡

When Something Changes Everything

Your change will move at a snail's pace if you allow the old culture to run the new show.

What worked for the past becomes the enemy of the new day. We are hard wired into old cultures, habits, timetables and ways. When we change, we experience little shocks as old habits short-circuit. But if you withstand the initial shock of doing it differently, even learning to appreciate the sensations of a new adventure, you will succeed in changing and healing. This is the essence of being resilient.

You'll experience the aftershocks of change regardless. It's best to feel them as you move toward the new reality.

Live Tomorrow More Than Yesterday

Once you've sifted through the ashes of the past and recovered what matters, be guided by where you now need to go rather than where you've been.

Some Middle Eastern tribes give members new names and ways of dressing as they mature through the seasons of their lives. This process invites them to recreate themselves internally as they adjust externally five times in the course of a life. It is logical, isn't it?

In many tribal societies, following the death rites for a spouse, the widowed one is taken to a solitary place and allowed to mentally and emotionally unload their past. Then, when they return to the tribe, they live in a new place.

When something changes everything, we need to prepare for what we are becoming more than what we've been.

What's the point of preparing for the past?

Peter McGugan

Become The Vision

Cultural change is upsetting, disorienting, and can make you feel like you are drifting.

There needs to be a destination that captures your imagination—a vision that holds everyone's attention and kisses hearts.

If negative self-talk echoes in your head, imagine your mind as a radio. Close your eyes and focus in on the dial. Change the station so you're listening to positive thoughts.

Tune into the love channel in your mind.

You can talk yourself into or out of anything.

Expect Casualties

Unless people see their place in your new future, they may sabotage your journey. If they will be in your future life, explain how, and reassure them. Reality has begun a new chapter and you are adapting.

People who loved your past might oppose a different future for you. They'd rather support an illusion.

If you devote your life to deifying and preserving the past, a few sweet people who fear change can go on pretending.

The people who truly love you, want your life to be full and fun and complete. They'll encourage you to move toward a sweet future.

Those who try to hold you back may threaten to let go if you change. To get a grip on yourself you may need to let go of them.

➡

If you keep all the people who were in your life before everything changed, it's either a miracle or a sure sign you aren't changing.

Find A Living Example

Find yourself a strong role model. Through your support group, PTA, religion or a national association, find a friend/mentor who is living your dream.

Offer to buy them coffee or a meal and ask a few of your most pressing questions. People don't mind being asked questions by anyone who wants an honest answer.

No matter where you are, if you can post a letter, you can find a friend. One amazing benefit of the Internet is it extends your back fence around the world. Being able to go online and find people who've been through it themselves, can offer insightful and quick answers wherever you are.

People in small communities or the countryside have a much tougher time with loss because there is little support. The Internet can be a link when little else is available.

SEE: **WHAT'S NEXT?**

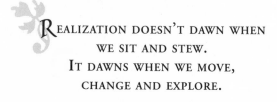

REALIZATION DOESN'T DAWN WHEN
WE SIT AND STEW.
IT DAWNS WHEN WE MOVE,
CHANGE AND EXPLORE.

Peter McGugan

Career Change, Loss Of A Job

Anger, rejection, grief, confusion, panic, relief and freedom accompany career changes. People in today's work force will change industries, employers and products more than any generation before. Employment is much more liquid than in your parents' time, so avoid comparing your career's stability with that of another era.

The '90s have seen greedy stockholders profit from huge layoffs, and a year later companies hire people for reorganized divisions.

When organizations try to change, only 20 percent of the employees are change friendly; 80 percent are resistant. As American corporations must reinvent themselves to survive, they eliminate employees who've done it the old way, reorganize divisions and then hire people eager to do the new job being offered.

Change is challenging.

In the next decade more than half of the work force will be working out of the home. At this moment, you may be more on trend than unemployed.

North America is experiencing a quiet workers' revolt. As mother corporations become 'Mutha' corporations that earn profits, pay CEOs obscenely, freeze wages, and lay people off, the casualty is corporate loyalty.

No wonder we've fallen out of love with bigness.

In response to the end of a corporation's investment in its people, liberated workers are finding indepen-

➡

When Something Changes Everything

dence, joining smaller organizations or becoming their own CEO in their spare room, the "virtual office."

WHEN THE MOTHER BIRD
PUSHES THE BABIES OUT OF THE NEST,
THEY TUMBLE TO THE GROUND
AND LAY THERE WAITING TO DIE
OR THEY SPREAD THEIR WINGS
AND DISCOVER THEY CAN FLY.

Peter McGugan

Strategies For Successful Career Changes

- Honestly look at what happened and what the lessons are for you. Put your bruised ego aside so you can study and own the lessons this experience offers.

- List all the opportunities you have now. You are surrounded by potentials. They are the gifts of change. Build on them.

- Explore the marketplace with the people already in it. Learn where dollars are flowing, what's hot, what's not and what's next. Read, research, have the customer's experience, interview, analyze and become a leading expert in the problems of this time. Examine what's happening now and what's coming next and position yourself as the solution.

- Buy experts lunches and learn how to get into the game.

- Avoid advice from people who know nothing about where you want to be.

- Trust that one day in the future, you will look back and be thankful for the change you are in the midst of now. All change feels like chaos as it happens.

SEE: **READER PATH: CAREER CHANGE, LOSS OF A JOB**

When Something Changes Everything

Changing

List six characteristics that describe the person you want to be and post this on your bathroom mirror.

1. _____

2. _____

3. _____

4. _____

5. _____

6. _____

The way to change is to get up out of that chair and become the person you want to be.

To become it, be it.

Peter McGugan

Change Master Skills

A Change Master is good at Life: To be good at Life is to be good with change.

As your group's change manager, it is important for you to regard and honor the past; and after a time of remembering and mourning, you can signal it is time to align the organization, its structure and home, with the needs of tomorrow.

Most of this book is compassionately written to identify a personal moment and gently offer you insight, companionship or a nudge.

This is a graduate course in survival. As Charles Darwin said, "It is not the strongest of the species that survive, nor the most intelligent, but the most responsive to change."

These are assertiveness skills for the managers of changing organizations and families.

1. Clean House
Defuse the emotional bombs of the old culture.

If we don't clean house, emotional detonators linger in dark corners and there isn't room for newness. People get snagged on shards of the past.

Change the art, move the furniture, get rid of needless stuff that only supports the old system's way of doing things. Clean out the closets.

When Something Changes Everything

These are powerful passages that are necessary and never as bad as we think they will be. As with so many things, the anticipation is more painful than actually going through it. You can make this a sweet tribute by doing it with your team. There will be memories, laughs and tears. It is a special time.

You'll feel good for having dispersed things for charities to utilize. Your transition into the new phase will have clearly begun and the new images of change around you will help your people make necessary internal changes.

2. Change Your Ways

THE OLD CULTURE IS DESIGNED TO SUPPORT ITSELF, NOT BRING ABOUT ITS OWN END.

Your reinvention will move at a snail's pace if you allow the historic culture to run today.

People are habitual and get wired into old cultures, habits, ways and timetables.

Severing connections with what used to work is frightening. The fabric of the past is easier to visualize than the future, but hanging onto the thread of an unraveling past is much riskier than weaving yourself into a beautiful future.

Change your ways and suddenly you will have your own attention and be earning your own respect. Confidence will rise and enthusiasm will follow.

You'll own each new day and the void will shrink.

Everyone will experience the aftershocks of change. It's best to feel them as you're moving toward a bright future.

As they are severed, connections spark emotional bursts. Be a sensitive, strong, forward-looking parent and example.

3. Find Living Examples

Find strong role models who understand the path you're on, people whose experience gives them a view of the big picture and the holes in the road.

While you are being strong and people lean on you, you'll need someone to lean on—a source of solid advice and confidence.

How have others managed such a change? Join an association or support group and befriend people in the know.

Offer to buy mentors a meal and ask your "advisory board" a few of your most pressing questions. People don't mind being asked questions by anyone who respects an honest answer. Always show appreciation and if the insights are valuable, ask if they'll be a 911 advisor.

➡

No matter where you are, if you can post a letter, you can find an advisor. The Internet extends your back fence around the world. Going online and finding people who've been through it themselves can offer insightful and quick answers wherever you may be.

Business people in small communities or the countryside have a much tougher time because there are fewer support options. The Internet is an amazing link.

4. Hang Onto The Future.

Once you've sifted through the cold ashes of the past, aim yourself where you want to go, not where you've been.

By doing the exercises in this book, you develop what's next.

The most powerful way to make it happen is by creating a vision journal. Gather thoughts, photos, articles, magazine pictures and information about the future you're moving toward. Thoughts are powerful things and organizing them in an album turbocharges their power. It keeps you focused on the bigger picture and the right prize.

Your job, as your own change manager, is to champion the vision by communicating and promoting it to your team.

People who've enjoyed the old organization may sabotage change. For them it is more convenient to live on as a relic of the past, a sweet memento of the good old days.

This is paralysis. To align yourself with what has died is a choice of doom.

Peter McGugan

So your job is to find each person's carrot—the prize they want badly enough to change for. Promote the adventure using beautiful pictures of their carrot and stoke the fires of passion with excitement.

Without a destination, we stay put. But to get to a place of greater comfort and happiness, we'll commit to changing.

Sell the journey so people will clearly understand it and the payoff it holds for them. If individuals can't see how this future works for their values and goals, they won't invest with you. You'll be struggling to engineer a new future, while surrounded by saboteurs.

Post photographs of the destination, motivating phrases or mottos for all to see. Keep a fresh flow of these motivators coming. Put reminders on your desk, your refrigerator and especially on your bathroom mirror.

These are the focusing tools that will move you and others, most confidently, in the direction of the dream.

The old saying, "Be careful what you ask for, because you'll get it," is very true—unless what you are asking for is the past.

➡

5. Be The Hero Of Your Story

Tragedy either burns the passion out of people or it forges heroes.

If you've read this far and feel excitement about the possibilities, you contain a hero.

Any Life that includes investment will include classroom time in the school of hard knocks. Give expression to the part of you that has learned from this experience and been forged stronger.

Because you are reading these words, recognize that you are a survivor and that is the core of a leader.

6. Seize Control Of The Schools

To release the old culture of its stranglehold, seize control of the schools. This is a basic step of revolutionaries.

Training must be redirected to serve the needs of tomorrow, not the ego of yesterday.

Compile a list of the many idea generators (schools) affecting your people and sensitively determine how each can be aligned to fuel the future.

Move too fast on this and you may trigger a mutiny. Every ship needs an anchor, and sacred symbols of the past need to remain.

Some people have great difficulties letting go. Loyalty is among their highest values, abandonment among their worst fears.

Each person needs individual help and consideration with the process of changing.

Peter McGugan

7. Avoid The Teeth Of Gossip Mills

Fear and uncertainty fuel rumor mills, threats and sabotage. Frightening the frightened is easy sport for the weak.

Save your mental energy for the facts and focus on growing solutions rather than fear and confusion.

8. Identify Your Currency

What is each person willing to change for? Is their currency adventure, involvement, money, security, a house with a swimming pool, new customers, a fresh image and identity?

WE CHANGE BEHAVIOR
WHEN WE EARN TANGIBLE PAYOFFS QUICKLY.

Structure each day so everyone moves toward the desired result.

When we know the currency we're after, we measure true success rather than the sideline stuff.

Focusing on the big picture of what you want helps organize the days.

Your true priorities are now becoming organized into your daily focus. Get what you need more of while avoiding unmanageable debt and impossible promises.

Just as inaction is hard when you are starving, it's hard to argue with success when you measure it in currency.

Ultimately, change lives or dies by the flow of currency.

➡

When Something Changes Everything

9. Reinvent Your Reward Systems

If you don't change the reward systems, you'll reward resistance.

Because we feel sorry for ourselves, we reward our own pitifulness. While we're doing the hard work of grieving, we'll reward ourselves with all kinds of treats and sweets. And since we're giving ourselves so many of our favorite things, we'll stay sad and over indulgent. This vicious cycle must be escaped.

Imagine yourself in five years if you keep indulging self-pity. Is this a downward spiral?

Put rewards for anything but actions that contribute to the new reality out of reach. Avoid contaminating the accomplishment-based reward system by giving treats when they are undeserved. Treats are deserved when we've adapted to change.

Talk about and reward actions that shoulder responsibility for driving the change.

If behavior hasn't changed enough, make bigger changes to your reward systems.

On days you don't work at the change, get angry and punish yourself. Spend the night on the couch. Discipline yourself the way you would discipline a lazy teenager!

The sooner you adjust your reward system, the sooner you'll be comfortable with what you awake to each day.

10. Expand Your Knowledge Base

Moving into new territory creates doubts, suspicion and fears. These paralyzers feed on ignorance.

Crank up the communication on every level! Journal your thoughts, fears and feelings. Examine them and douse burning fears with the knowledge available from books, tapes, support groups, professional associations, the Internet or any other means that will give you answers and confidence.

Know the questions and go in search of the answers. The resource guide in this book may be the starting place.

The self-talk in your head is crucial. Be sure the thoughts you allow to linger and your internal statements support the honest truth about the day and the change you wish to make.

If negative thoughts blast your head, imagine your mind as a radio. Relax into this image and once you have it, change the station so you're listening to positive thoughts.

Tune into the love channel in your mind.

You can talk yourself into or out of anything.

➡

11. Expect Casualties

People who loved the past will oppose a different future for you. They'd rather you align with what was, to support their grief and inflexibility.

If you devote your life to deifying and preserving memories, a few sweet people who don't manage change can pretend; and you will exist as a historical animatron. You will barely exist. Your organization will be at great risk.

Those who apply negative labels, use threats and hold you back are telling you they are willing to let go if you change. And those fair-weather folks, who don't understand what has happened to you and the recovery process you're in, will be of little use or comfort now.

Communicate the truth and whys of your thoughts.

If you keep all the people who were in your life before everything changed, it's a miracle or a sure sign you aren't adjusting.

Earthquakes have aftershocks.

12. Communicate, Communicate And Do It Some More

Normal communication with yourself and others isn't enough. There needs to be a lot of self-talk, a lot of research and a lot of listening and mutual planning.

Standard communication efforts won't cut it now.

People need to hear and see your rationale and logic for changing. They'll want to know what's coming and how it will include them.

Communication is the lubricant of recovery.

Give yourself permission to be really excited while listening to others' opinions.

Peter McGugan

When you are dealing with children and coworkers, become a cheerleader and rally participation. Listen to advice from your experts; ignore what people who've never been there, who've never tried, have to say. The reasons they give you for not going for it are the beliefs that straightjacket lives.

Commit to being a student of what you want to become; listen to voices of experience and be ready to adjust your course, to back off and rethink things before moving forward again.

13. Support Your Decision Makers

While top management is frantically trying to salvage and save what's left, too often the people who'll benefit from success become troublesome thorns.

Just as it is easier for a soldier to be recognized and promoted during times of battle, it is easier for you to score points during chaos. Learn and use the new rules as they form and reform. Be understanding and supportive as the organization finds its way through the maze of change and you will make a big difference in your future.

Change squeezes people, and whatever they contain spews out. While others release their inner uglies, show the best of what you're made of.

➡

14. Transformation Is Life!

Nothing stays the same.

Death, births and evolution are the inhaling and exhaling of the Cosmos—the breath of Life.

To be a change master requires forgiveness and surrender to the change-force operating within everything you perceive.

Change doesn't happen to people and things—it is the core of them. Change is the melody of atoms and neutrons.

Consistency is the perception of the ignorant.

The change master's response to living is to blend acceptance, resiliency, faith, hope, hunger, courage, wisdom and grace into a living awareness.

Change masters awake each day, knowing change happens.

SEE: **READER PATH: MANAGEMENT**

Chemical Dependency

The popular misconception is that chemicals make hurt and fear go away.

They don't.

Chemicals just put a lid on feelings so, for a time, feelings can't drift up to your consciousness. Thoughts and feelings are as powerful as steam. In time the lid on your heart will crack and blow.

Rotted old contaminated feelings leak out as rage, phobias, nastiness, workaholism, addictions, eating disorders, failed relationships, depressions and illness.

Conservative estimates say one in ten people are dependant on alcohol, drugs or both. If you have even a small suspicion you rely on chemicals, or if someone has observed it, begin to change.

Liberation is exhilaration.

Guidance and companionship will shed the light on the cauldron of anguish, confusion and fear you've become.

To truly satisfy the hungers of your spirit and fill yourself with what you truly need to feel full, see the resource guide in this book and make some calls.

*Wherever you are, Alcoholics Anonymous or Narcotics Anonymous have created paths. Observe one of their meetings.

SEE: **BALANCE AND IMBALANCE,
DRUGS, RESOURCE GUIDE**

When Something Changes Everything

Children And Grief

In our efforts to protect and shield children, we teach them ignorance about death and grief. Many children have learned by osmosis that death is a squeamish adult topic, a taboo.

As parents' hearts are shattered by grief, the comprehension and reasoning processes of children are often forgotten.

Children And Blame

The world of children revolves around responsibility, and usually when there is big messy trouble in the house, a child had something to do with it. Damage, destruction and upsets must be apologized for, the wrong doer punished; then, following penance, all is well.

Children, in the midst of death or tragedy, blame themselves. When someone dies, a child may silently believe something they did made this bad thing happen.

If they don't blame themselves or a sibling, they may blame God, refusing to forgive or pray, even hating this father of destruction that broke their family.

Each child needs to be asked why they feel in their heart that this thing happened.

Peter McGugan

Tell Me Again

The open mind of a child absorbs information. As volumes of data are added to awareness, a child's ability to perceive, recognize, associate and understand, balloons. "Tell me again about…" is a child's way of asking for a vitally important event to be reoffered and reentered with a new level of cognizance or awareness.

While this may not be easy or convenient for a grieving adult, it is necessary for the child's relationship with the event and all those affected.

Lies We Grow Up Believing

• We were read stories that ended with "They lived happily ever after." On some base levels we may believe this. Children are fascinated with death and funerals; but they're often made to feel this interest is morbid, dirty and unhealthy.

• Adults confuse children with terms like "passed away," "put to sleep" or "lost," giving the impression that death is temporary.

• These seemingly innocent experiences are the seeds of life-long handicaps that leave us unequipped when death scrambles our lives.

10 Ideas For Parenting A Grieving Child

1. Use direct and clear terms when discussing death.

2. Children need to be fluent in the language of feelings. Teach them the names for feelings like confusion, guilt, jealousy and how to use these feelings productively. Encourage them to learn the names of what they are feeling. Then you can communicate what you are feeling and why. Our culture is remiss in teaching the language of the heart.

3. One on one, with your full attention, ask each child to, from time to time, explain his or her understanding of the accident, illness or death. Allow each child to communicate their depth of understanding to you. Be certain they are not blaming themselves or a sibling.

4. A fascination with death is an education for healthy living, not a morbid obsession. Allow mock funerals to happen. Children recreating funeral rituals are interpreting the experience. Seek age-appropriate books or tapes to help each child understand and grieve.

5. Teach children there are inappropriate and appropriate times for crying and rage. During grief, emotional swings and rage are appropriate. Teach them to vent in ways that do not hurt others. (See "anger" section)

Peter McGugan

6. Talks with adults are very important; be patient and available. Talks with other children and how they cope with loss are equally important. Gather grieving children so they can work through it together.

7. Invite children to express their feelings and fears regularly. Reality for a child is the world as she/he perceives it today. That world can be altered or twisted by a few words or a bad dream

8. Avoid martyrdom. It indicates sick or dead people are more special and loved than the living and the strong. A child's resentment of the sick, injured or deceased makes complicated emotions more toxic.

9. Sadness descends like the Hindenburg. For you the cemetery may be the place to release emotions, but children may resent being taken to a strange place that has nothing to do with memories. A child may grieve best at the ice cream parlor that is filled with memories. Be sensitive.

10. Be a good observer. A definite change in behavior, in any direction, is a potential problem. A child who loses the adventurous spirit, suddenly behaves too perfectly, or acts out aggression is a child struggling with rage and guilt. Seek guidance from a grief counselor.

Children In Crisis

Children are honest mirrors. They reflect their environment.

If you need a child to change, first find the courage and honesty to look in your own mirror.

If you resent the pressures and responsibilities of your miserable adult life, is it surprising your child rejects the advice and scripts you want them to follow?

Rebellious children clearly say, "I don't take your advice because I think I'm better at life than you are. I'm more interesting, I have better friends, I have more fun."

Teenagers use drugs and gangs to belong, or to escape what they dread becoming.

Life is the point!

If your adult life is all work and then more work with no time for play or celebration, the rebellious child may be saving itself from your script.

To heal the relationship with the child, begin by healing your relationship with Life. Sweeten your life experiences and you will be in a better place to negotiate with your child. Invite them to join you for mutual fun.

People do not change because we tell them to, they change through a desire to move to a place of less pain.

- Libraries and bookstores contain solutions for the specific problems you face. Ignorance fuels conflicts and fear.

Peter McGugan

- Resiliency is strongest in the young. They rebound and learn quickly.

- Mental health centers or continuing education often offer parenting classes.

Difficulties In School

- Children with problems in school need evaluation. Their school, the local college or university can recommend a specialist. You might also investigate the Learning Disability Association of America, 4126 Library Road, Pittsburgh PA, 15234; phone (412) 341-1515.

- Tutoring can make a great difference. Check the yellow pages under "tutoring."

Child Loss

The most difficult of all losses, when hello means goodbye, is the most mystifying piece of God's puzzle.

It is life's cruelest turn. Unaware that there is no baby, a mother's milk comes in. The ache in the bosom is a profound physical manifestation of the confusion and pain.

Gone too soon, the brief, bright lives of child angels often offer the greatest inspiration, courage and lessons. They teach profound lessons.

When a child is gone, parents assume the child is adrift, rather than safely back at the bosom of Creation.

The grieving parent—God's short-changed protector of this tiny soul—sends awareness out to the child so the little soul may be wrapped in the parent's consciousness.

With so much consciousness projected out to the child, there is little left in the parent's body but wretched disappointment and exhaustion.

Most of this book is written for you. But it is not enough. Find a support group.

Only the people who are going through it can say the things you need to hear.

Peter McGugan

For angels
who've run back to the lap of God,
heaven is home.

SEE: READER PATH: LOSS OF A CHILD, ANGER,
HOW GREAT PEOPLE HANDLE LOSS,
FRIENDS, SOUL RECOVERY

When Something Changes Everything

Rites For The Most Private Passage

The loss of an infant is considered an intimate crisis of the parents and immediate family. Society does not respond.

Here are some ideas grieving parents have suggested for you.

- Name the baby.

- Respect the baby's body and go through a ritual— cremation and scattering the ashes or burial. Scatter the petals of the flowers people sent.

- Make your own service. Play music you listened to together during the pregnancy.

- Write the baby letters including all the things you didn't have time to say.

- Plant a tree or flower garden.

- Be extremely patient with the way you and your spouse deal with this. Join a group and get marriage counseling to understand more about what you're going through.

This is an important passage in your life that does not impact on your friends and family the way it does on you. They did not have a relationship with the baby's soul the way you did.

SEE: **REVERSE THE SITUATION**

Peter McGugan

Child Loss Support

- Compassionate Friends is a national support group with more than 700 local chapters. They offer understanding, support, referrals and information. Their address is P.O. Box 3696, Oak Brook, IL 60522-3696.

- Childhood cancer foundations, often called Candlelighters, offer families assistance and counseling. The national number is (800) 366-2223, or (301) 657-8401.

SEE: RESOURCE GUIDE

A Story
Following the loss of her firstborn children, twin girls, Canadian broadcaster Leigh Morrow made her own beautiful card announcing the births and deaths of her daughters.

Making these cards was very therapeutic for her.

"It allowed me to write my daughters' names over and over again, confirming their birth and acknowledging I would seldom write their names again."

"These carefully chosen names had served a much shorter purpose than I had ever imagined."

Because my friend acknowledged their lives to the world, the world could acknowledge back.

When Something Changes Everything

Climbing

True, there is a climb ahead, but isn't that what Life promises with every morning? We have to climb out of bed and move upward. We must climb to reach the special moments I call sweet spots in time. Sweet spots...those glorious moments we Love what is happening around us enough to forget pain and allow our spirits to soar and fly. Sweet spots happen when you forgive Life for the difficult lessons, the losses, the imposed sacrifices and the climbs. Sweet spots happen when you're right with the world.

Think about that expression: right with the world. It implies the world has always been right, but we haven't been right with it.

When we're right with the world, we forgive change.

FORGIVE LIFE.
IT NEVER, EVER PROMISED FOREVER.

Peter McGugan

Codependency

Trying to control someone else is folly. It leads to frustration, anger, abuse and depression.

We cannot save people from themselves. Often we try to change other people so we can delay fixing ourselves.

Joining them on their slide to bottoming out offers company for our own misery and distraction from the responsibility of our own story.

Fix your own story and then let them fix theirs. By saving yourself you create a healing path that they may eventually follow you onto.

We teach best by example.

This is a challenging process. Codependents hate to let a loyal and validating pity partner fly free. They will try to sabotage you.

This book will accompany you through many moments but Codependents Anonymous, Nar-Anon or Al-Anon will show you paths to liberation and offer worthy companions for the journey.

Conflicts

As the dust settles, we must adjust ourselves to an all encompassing reality. We must reinvent our relationship with an alien future. This is a creative and disturbing process.

When you are on pins and needles with yourself, clashes with friends, family, loved ones, bosses and coworkers are to be expected. As you adjust for your new reality, others don't know what to do or say. Often it's the wrong thing.

You cannot expect anyone else to adjust at the same moments in the same ways you do.

As Kahlil Gibran teaches us, "Allow space in your togetherness."

Conflict Resolutions

• Reference your support system and keep variety in the people you talk with and the places you go.

• Write a list of your top values for today and tomorrow. Uncertainty can make you confused.

• Read about anger and avoid misplacing it.

• Men and women often grieve differently. Inquire about and honor the other's process while staying focused on your own.

• Often one partner is consistently strong for the other. But everyone needs to be weak with someone.

Peter McGugan

- See a therapist or join a therapy group if you feel stuck, overwhelmed or isolated.

- Recovery involves the most intimate aspects of your heart, faith, illusions, hopes and dreams. Much of this reorganizing of your inner pantry must be done during private moments. You need time alone with the loss.

- You need to wail, cry and purge the sounds and tears of the wounded. When a rescuer/comforter says, "There, there, don't cry," they intercept this natural expression and healing. Tell them to just let you cry. And if they cry too, for your reasons or their own, you'll both be better for it.

- You will need a variety of people to talk with. If you lean too heavily on just one crutch, it may snap.

- Life and people get absurd; remember to laugh. Laughter and crying have similar therapeutic effects. Our bodies shake tensions and feelings loose, and we release them through sounds. A good laugh session can be as therapeutic as a good cry.

- Seek people going through similar changes. Get guidance for the group from a counselor.

- When relationships become troubled, a counselor can help you make adjustments. Ask friends, your mental health association or a hospital to recommend three. Choose the one you both prefer.

SEE: **ANGER, VIOLENCE AND REVENGE, WAR, RESOURCE GUIDE**

Crime And Revenge

Anarchy, theft, rape and murder are too often crimes committed by a grieving soul. The loss of the tribe, the end of the agricultural era's interwoven community and the loss of strong father/mother parenting teams create generations unequipped to manage their own grief. Rather than having their own internal rage and grief process, they vent their rage at society, the defenseless and God.

Shoplifting among affluent widowed females is alarmingly common.

The reasons may be: "Something changed everything and left a huge void in my life, in my heart. I'm in unbearable pain and the world just goes merrily on. And I didn't do anything to deserve this punishment and pain! Now I want what I deserve. I want to even the score."

The grieving don't think straight.

We say people are "out of their right minds with grief."

In this confused, blinded state, people often do not see the consequences of actions. The world is a blur; nothing is as real or solid as it was before.

But revenge doesn't work. It complicates and prolongs recovery. If you understand the concept of karma—that what you inflict unto others, will be done back to you—revenge sets you up for a very, very long recovery.

We exist to evolve our level of consciousness by consuming experiences—both happy and sad.

Peter McGugan

The life master chooses love and faith, peace and potentials. Life masters cherish what was and what is, as they go on.

Criminal reactions to loss are a violent scream for help, attention, love and help.

With murder it is the survivors who suffer most.

If you sense yourself stretching the rules of society or thinking about criminal acts of revenge, STOP!

STOP!

The fates of people who've done this kind of crime are worse than what you are living.

If you have lost your relationship with someone— committing a crime will cost you your relationship with EVERYONE!

The price of revenge is loss of freedom, intimacy, respect, potentials and dignity. It costs everything and everyone you have and more. It costs you what you would have had.

It leaves you with less than nothing.

If you are inclined to break society's rules, if you feel a cry for help building inside you, find a place where caring people will hear you. Cry out very loud and release what you've been thinking.

Go today to a hospital, recovery group or therapist and find the care, structure and support you need. Drugs will not resolve this, but talking it out and acting it out in a healing way will make it better.

Destruction, theft or revenge are never solutions.

SEE: **RESOURCE GUIDE**

When Something Changes Everything

Crime Violation

Coping with crime creates profound changes in your life. In its wake, issues of faith, security, pain and fear are common.

Avoid victim mentality. People who perpetrate crimes are the true victims of their actions. The ramifications on the injured parties, however profound, are easier to heal than a criminal soul. Criminals vent their desperate rage through destruction. If you're now full of that rage, who gave it to you? And if your rage grows into hatred and violence, who wins you as a convert, the forces of goodness or evil?

Try the following with a wise friend or a therapist:

- Make a list of what it will take to make you feel safe again. Then make it a reality.

- If you block the event from memory or can't describe it calmly, you are containing emotions. The feelings can build within you like a bomb waiting to explode. Avoid this by playing the memory of the event as if it were a videotape in your mind. Describe every detail out loud to someone. Feel all the feelings. Then play it again and again until remembering it vividly no longer packs emotional dynamite. This defuses the incident.

Peter McGugan

- Culture your sense of confidence. If you are living in a crime belt, learn to live happily with it or learn to leave it. There are safe havens in the world.

- If there is a future trial, focus on it intensely. Ponder, think, prepare and journal until you are exhausted. Then pass the information on to someone who cares and love the ones you're with. Repeat as necessary.

- Nurture renewal and confidence.

- More information is available through the National Organization for Victim Assistance, 1757 Park Road N.W., Washington, DC 20010; phone (202) 232-6682.

Crying Real Tears

The architect who designed you created tears of joy and tears of sorrow. Grieving tears differ from tears that lubricate your eyes. Researchers have discovered the stress chemicals that tighten up your face are released by crying. Facial muscles, filled with the stress chemicals, tighten and then quiver just before we release stress through tears. Each swallowed emotion, each denied tear, ferments within you.

Crying also releases endorphins that comfort you. So when you tear up, let them flow.

Peter McGugan

Dangers In The Zero Zone

Zero is often what is in your brain now.

Alert yourself to reality. When traveling, fill your mind with consciousness of your surroundings. The risk of traffic accidents is four times higher among families that are grieving.

Loss cultivates loss.

Don't put yourself and other innocent people and children at risk.

When you need to move, visit a place of nature, a shoreline or park, and wander in this safe zone.

Nature will embrace you. We do not stay angry in nature.

SEE: ZERO ZONE, SHOPPING IN THE ZERO ZONE

FINDING A SAFE PLACE
AND LYING DOWN
IS A GOOD IDEA
DURING AN EARTHQUAKE.

Death Of A Spouse

Until you are without them, you cannot imagine your love to be so vast. The void is oceanic.

Almost every passage in this book was written for you.

The loss of a spouse includes the loss of identity, security and purpose. The first year following the death is your most risky time as an adult. More adults die within the first year of losing a spouse than at any other time.

You have a contract with Creation, and there is loving and living for you to do. You are still here because there is something left for you to experience or share.

Do you have a sense of it?

It helps to make a list of all the purposes you recognize for yourself. Think of friends, children or grandchildren.

If your purpose for going on isn't clear, launch a search. This world is starving for many things. There is no shortage of reasons to live when you look beyond your front door.

Make a list of your abilities and contact a volunteer organization.

It is important to stay in charge of your life. Learn the skills your spouse used to do and avoid letting wellwishing people take over.

Avoid making hasty decisions. Special things you collected together may trigger pain. If you wish, put them away. A year from now they may give you warm feelings and a link to your history.

Cherish yourself. We must all learn to parent, love and forgive ourselves...to live with ourselves. Take yourself on special outings and give yourself the care you deserve.

We crave touch, so have yourself pampered. Get a hair style, a massage, manicure or facial. Be touched.

The crying you do produces endorphins that comfort you, and the tears release the toxins produced by stress.

You're not going crazy if strange sightings or sensings happen. You have seeking behavior. You'll expect to see them watching the television, or you'll see them from the corner of your eye.

Sensing them is a normal part of the process. When you feel your spouse's presence, encourage them to go into The Light where they are empowered and protected.

Encouraging them to move to that phase helps you both. Doing this will only enhance your continuing sense of them.

When you miss them most, write a letter, saying the things you need to say. Put it in a special place and three months later have a look at it. You do resolve things and change.

Although it may not seem so, you do move forward.

➡

When Something Changes Everything

* If you feel adrift, there are recovery programs available through places of worship, continuing education and The Widowed Persons Service, which has more than 200 chapters nationwide. Address: 1909 K Street N.W., Washington, DC 20049.

SEE: READER PATH: DEATH OF A SPOUSE,
ANGER, HOLDING ON, THIRD ENERGY,
HOW GREAT PEOPLE HANDLE LOSS,
FRIENDS, PARTNERS,
SOUL RECOVERY,

Depression

Following loss, depression is logical and understandable. The ingredients, anger, confusion, obsession, exhaustion and listlessness, naturally shadow traumatic change.

The startling realization that we attract, have and hold and release everything in our lives, gives us a WHOP on the side of the head. When Life isn't easy, it really isn't easy.

Depression always involves anger turned inward. It is very important to understand the anger you contain.

Make a list of all the people and situations you are angry with. Include things you have not forgiven yourself for.

Look at that list and decide what you can do to fix each situation.

If you can't fix it, your choice is to continue carrying it or to let it go. Read more about anger.

Exercise allows your body to release its natural mood-lifting drugs. Try walking. Choose a safe place, no traffic, and your body will deliver a natural high.

Years of depression following loss indicate ineffective grieving and a refusal to begin a new life.

Depression is a deep hole we must climb out of. The climb requires choice, nutrition, exercise, thought, prayer and concentrated effort; and the rewards are the sweetest Life offers.

SEE: ANGER, QUICK FIXES,
CHEMICAL DEPENDENCY

Differences In Grieving:
Emotional Versus Physical

Understanding emotional versus physical clarifies why people grieve so differently.

The emotional person lives life with the attitude "I feel, therefore I am."

Loss plunges emotional people into the maze of their own feelings and spirit. We emotionals then feel our way out of the maze, and into the Light.

It is wet and lonely work but we know it is the only way out of the pain and confusion.

The physical person lives life dealing with stuff. Their concern is not how anything feels but whether it functions.

In the unfamiliar territory of emotions, the physical person gets angry, blames, rants and possibly pushes, works, builds, buys, or travels their way around the feelings.

———

Grieving styles are intimate, private and quirky.

Allow others their creative process. Share what is working for you, and let them tell you what worked for them today. I believe everyone needs a support group to talk the process out with.

It is not important to witness, match or share another person's grieving. It is just important to know everyone has their outlets.

Peter McGugan

Difficult Days

Ten Things That Help

1. Cry first, think later.

2. Exercise.

3. Write a ballad, a poem or journal.

4. Write letters.

5. Clean something.

6. Garden.

7. Call some friends.

8. Go for a walk in nature.

9. See a film.

10. Repeat steps 1 through 9.

Ten Things That DON'T Help

1. Deny it is a difficult day.

2. Hold back the tears.

3. Hurt or abuse yourself or anyone else.

4. Stalk someone or seek revenge.

5. Be with insensitive people.

6. Get drunk.

7. Take mood-altering drugs.

8. Eat unhealthy amounts of food.

9. Stay shut off from life after a good cry.

10. Run to your parents.

When Something Changes Everything

Disasters

Wind battered, we dangle from a thread of faith, clutching a seed of hope.

Grow that seed of hope with your thoughts and actions and the help of your community. Where there is no kindness, invite it.

- Seek worthy guides who've carved a path through this experience. Ask the police, fire fighters, go online or contact a newsroom and ask for names of people who've been through a similar disaster.

- Your story encourages your community to blossom with kindness. As the recipient, you are the teacher. Be this with grace and without shame. From one ugly moment we can grow a thousand beautiful ones.

- Seek the lessons.

- Prioritize your actions. What doesn't matter? Simplify, simplify and then simplify. Do this and you arrive at wisdom.

- An old proverb says, "Now that the roof has caved in, I have a beautiful view of the moon."

Peter McGugan

Disenchantment

Disenchantment is normal, understandable and human.

It is the dying of illusion.

Forgiveness means giving up all hopes of having a better past.

> LOSS IS LIFE'S GREATEST TEACHER.
> IT STERNLY GIVES US LESSONS
> ON HAVING AND HOLDING,
> ON HONORING LIFE AND LOVE.
> IT TEACHES US WHAT DOESN'T MATTER.

Being emotional and what our society would call "out of control" is not pleasant, but it is the way we were designed to respond to loss and you must go through the emotional swamp.

The word distress has a bad reputation. It is to dis-stress—to release stress. As long as other people and relationships are not being damaged, distress is the healing expression of emotions.

When you feel the need to distress, focus on the feelings and let them flow. Give the feelings full expression. Don't dilute these honest emotions with drugs that stagnate feelings within you. Let go!

SEE: **ANGER**

When Something Changes Everything

Drama Queens

The drama of loss is a potent elixir that draws a crowd. You become the surviving star of a tragedy.

All drama has three acts, a beginning, middle and an end.

When you've told the tale of your loss so many times you hear yourself sensationalizing it, making it more epic, the story is worn out.

That dog don't hunt.

Roll credits, drop the curtain!

If you tell your story to justify your weep and whimper, to stoke a warming fire of pity, it's time to make each day new and interesting for yourself and those who are still courageous enough to ask, "How was your day?"

Give yourself something good to report tomorrow.

Do the loss and gains exercise and develop new projects, experiences and adventures.

SEE: LOSS AND GAINS EXERCISE

MILK A COW ONLY 'TIL SHE'S ALMOST DRY.

Peter McGugan

Dreams

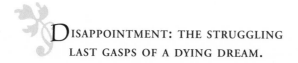

Disappointment: the struggling
last gasps of a dying dream.

If we believe that dreams have life, we must also allow
them death.

A gasping dream, sustained on a life support system,
mutates into a nightmare.

see: SLEEP PROGRAMMING

Drugs: Toxic Waste Dumps

For the grieving, there is no shortage of drugs and alcohol. These are the most popular numbing agents.

Because grieving requires time, tolerance and committed caring, our hurry-up-and-get-better culture leads us to a buffet of awareness blockers.

Being numbed will help you through a funeral or crisis, but the dependency needs to stop there.

From your inner Self you rebuild moment to moment. With this process you create a solid foundation for the next chapter of your life.

Medicine is not an exact science. A recovery rushed along by feeling-impairing drugs does not create a foundation.

The blustering winds of emotions are more ordered, exacting and healing than the tornadoes caused by drug dependencies. It is best to ride out the storm aware.

Tranquilizers are highly addictive. The following are some of the brand names for diazepam—Valium, Librium, Xanex, Halcyon...the list goes on and on.

If you're on drugs, take the bottles to a friendly pharmacist and ask what they are for. Don't take two drugs that have the same purpose. Doubling up is how people get hooked.

Be certain to ask the pharmacist if there would be problems if you stop taking one and consult your physician. If you don't get straight answers from your prescribing physician, get a second opinion.

Peter McGugan

You must take responsibility for your body. If you put your faith in drugs or alcohol, you'll lose a lot more than you've already lost.

SEE: CHEMICAL DEPENDENCY,
SLEEP PROGRAMMING

Dysfunctional Families

People who grew up with an addicted, abusive or violent parent or caregiver may fear the potentials of every next moment.

They fear movement, influence and change. Any person instigating change represents his or her ranting parent. The response is often to sabotage or hide at the first scent of change, whether it is positive or negative.

Living on pins and needles teaches us life can be a nauseating, out of control, roller coaster. Anyone assuming the role of change manager becomes the abuser.

If you are dealing with someone from a dysfunctional family, create stability and provide a lot of clear, slow communication. Offer choice, support and participation in a timetable they understand, so they can relax and trust this change process.

One resource for children of dysfunctional families is Adult Children of Alcoholics (ACOA) or Al-Anon. Find them in the white pages of your phone book.

SEE: **RESOURCE GUIDE**

Peter McGugan

Earth Angels

Most people want your pain gone, so they won't have to be generous of spirit, listening and caring, or face their own unresolved losses.

Grief is one of our culture's last taboos. It is barely fit for mainstream discussion.

When you are overwhelmed, find a place to sit and let the emotions flow. Be there a moment. The one who lifts you is your next encounter with an angel.

Often they appear from the fringes of our lives.

SEE: **FRIENDS, PEOPLE AT WORK, RESOURCE GUIDE**

Emergency Checklist

For the days you are a disaster area and the Red Cross is nowhere is sight,

Have you:

- ⭕ cried
- ⭕ forgiven yourself
- ⭕ cleaned yourself up
- ⭕ walked
- ⭕ written in your journal
- ⭕ eaten a healthy meal
- ⭕ exercised
- ⭕ been in nature
- ⭕ talked with friends
- ⭕ done something creative
- ⭕ seen a good film

Peter McGugan

Emotional Prisons

The unforgiving become outcasts of happiness, exiled from a past that no longer is and a future they refuse to embrace.

Anger, rage, guilt and fear are the four walls of the emotional prison.

Break through one wall into the Light, and the others weaken and crumble.

Endings And Beginnings

BEGINNINGS ARE EXCITING.
SLEEPING SENSES AWAKEN.
AND TIME SLOWS.
ENDINGS ARE EXCRUCIATING.
SLEEPING SENSES AWAKEN.
AND TIME SLOWS.

INTERNALLY, ONE PROCESS MIRRORS THE OTHER.
BOTH REFLECT A FULL LIFE.

Peter McGugan

Enemies

After a senseless act of destruction, we must vent anger in healthy ways again and again until we are exhausted.

If you read the following too soon after impact, you'll feel your rage rise.

Avoid reading this until the desire to forgive has kissed your heart.

Our worst enemies have been our greatest teachers here on Schoolhouse Earth, a boot camp for souls.

You are more alive, stronger, wiser, more compassionate and sensitive for having known your worst enemies.

They forced you to gulp Life rather than sip it. They force you to see more clearly, feel more deeply, to learn to grieve, to love and cherish with all your heart and to trust enough to let go.

Be grateful for your challenging teachers and the lessons they deliver. Without them you would not know, you would not be so awake.

Try this for just a moment to see how letting go of toxic hatred feels. Can you close your eyes and for a full minute send out a thank you message for the teachers in your life?

➡

When Something Changes Everything

How did that feel in your heart? Did you feel a stranglehold release, did you feel sludge melting away?

For that instant did your heart feel free?

Or did you simply read past the exercise, refusing to release the rage that is there?

Forgiveness requires distance and time from impact.

It washes your heart clean of sludge so it can beat strongly and love fully.

By forgiving, you liberate your spirit from the shroud of hate that destructive people want to cloak the world in. Don't let darkness in; don't let it win.

LIFE IS NOT MAN MADE.
YOU AND I ARE STUDENTS
OF SCHOOLHOUSE EARTH.
EVERYTHING IS A LESSON.
FORGIVE THE TEACHERS.

Peter McGugan

Escapes

Recovery from loss and change is intimate, moment to moment and inch by inch. It is a creative and personal odyssey we have unwillingly embarked upon.

It is part of your Ph.D. in Life.

Our culture sells escapes and diversions; but love, dreams and illusions are real. They occupy space in our beings. Ripped away, they leave wounds we must look at and tend, not just numb with chemicals or work.

To expect yourself to be over it tomorrow is like expecting a patient to jog away from the surgical table.

Healing requires energy and time.

Suppressed feelings, disillusionments and fears burrow deep in our being, fester there and then resurface in twisted, complicated ways.

The choice is to admit to and express the pain now or to contain it until it mutates and explodes.

Faith

THE MOTHER BIRD
PUSHES THE BABIES OUT OF THE NEST
BECAUSE SHE HAS FAITH THAT EACH WILL FLY.
THE BABIES FLY
BECAUSE SHE BELIEVED THEY WOULD.

Peter McGugan

Fault

Being accuser, judge and jury is not your job.

The wise and successful person, the person of higher faith, leaves evening the score to God.

You are not here to police the planet.

The price of hatred is far too high.

The law of our Universe is: What you give, you receive; what you do unto others shall be done to you. This is the central lesson of every one of the world's great religions.

It is the lesson of faith here on Schoolhouse Earth. The forgiver is freed through the forgiving.

The truth shadows all who destroy.

Let go and let God.

SEE: **TRIALS IN YOUR MIND**

Feeling Better

After months of grieving, the pain of the loss and its blue grey cloud feel normal. Misery is what we've become, the Self we now recognize. Pain is our umbilical cord to the past.

We must weather the emotional storm and when it lifts not wrap the grey clouds back around us.

After pain and turbulent emotions are exhausted, there are lovely moments when you feel beauty kiss your heart.

You're forgiving Life.

This ease can feel new, strange and disturbing.

To allow your spirits to soar because of excitement, a spring day or a new adventure is not abandonment. It is to arrive at a place where you can appreciate with clarity again.

Everyone who truly loves you wishes you the ability to forgive and live with easy smiles and peace-filled happy days.

If you refuse happiness when your heart reaches for it, you victimize yourself.

If you feel tremendous guilt over being happy, talk to caring and supportive friends who've gone through losses themselves.

Anyone who does not give you permission to be happy again isn't loving you.

SEE: **REVERSE THE SITUATION**

Peter McGugan

Firsts

The firsts are the aftershocks of your emotional earthquake. Seeing something for the first time since the loss, going to the old places, seeing a car like theirs, hearing the special song...all these things pinch your heart.

They are bittersweet moments we may flee from, or savor.

Each is a passage, a benchmark.

Second encounters carry less emotional artillery.

Feel and embrace each first. Ache and cry. This is your spirit's acknowledgment of something that was real.

Savor the firsts.

I HAD SOMETHING.
IT WAS VERY REAL,
I KNOW BECAUSE I FEEL.

Forgiveness

FORGIVENESS IS SURRENDERING ALL HOPE
OF PERFECTING THE PAST.

FORGIVENESS IS THE ENTRANCE
TO A PLACE OF LOVE.

IF WE DO NOT FORGIVE
WHAT WE DETEST THE MOST,
WE BECOME.

IT IS THE FORGIVER WHO IS FREED
THROUGH THE FORGIVING.

Peter McGugan

Friends

The people you shared fun and laughter with may not be close now. Your fun buddies may not recognize you now.

They feel inadequate and say the wrong things. They are not who you need.

Your fragility is distancing; expect more casualties.

Forgive them for their innocence. They cannot give what they do not have.

What you used to care about is trivial. Now you need sensitive, caring people. As the news of your loss travels, acquaintances you wouldn't have expected to hear from, people from the fringes of your life, will offer themselves. They aren't afraid to wade into the deepest pools of the emotional swamp. They've been there themselves.

Accept their friendship. They are your guides for a time.

As you drown in your swamp of grief, they will lift your head, mop your brow...listen.

When their life beckons, they must leave you...another loss.

And you are alone, to face the emptiness. To sit, angry, feeling abandoned unto yourself.

➡

When we've been alone long enough, we individually drag ourselves out of the emotional swamp and return to the living. You determine the timing. Some people stay in the emotional swamp a week, others stay a decade. Some, tragically, never leave.

If you are lacking loving, emotional friends, find a support group. Call your mental health association, hospital, church or Alcoholics Anonymous. Any of these will be able to refer you to a group that gently supports people through the experience you are having.

This is not a time to be angry at old friends who've stopped calling. It is a time to move toward people who understand.

SEE: **RESOURCE GUIDE**

Peter McGugan

Friends: How You Can Help Me Now

Dear _____:

Something changed everything.

And I have a lot of adjustments to make.
Some I'll do alone,
others I may do with you nearby.

Just listen.

When I need to think out loud,
you don't have to choose sides, justify why
or compare other people's stories to mine.

My thoughts come loaded with tears. Let me
release their weight freely.

As I sift through the ashes of my past,
I have contradictory moments.
Grief is not logical, it's emotional.

You don't have to cheer me up.

Let me know I'm loved,
and I'll work toward being fun again.

And then,
when something changes everything for you,
I'll be there.

Goals Of Recovering

Following impact, the events that changed everything are a thick, damp, blinding fog. Then...gradually it thins. It lifts and is only a gloomy mist on the mind.

Recovery's essence is to arrive at a place of ease with the truth about your past and the truth about your future. Once the pain and turbulent emotions are exhausted, there is clarity with living.

To want discomfort, fear and worry to end is not to abandon the people of your past, it is to abandon the fear, worry, and pain. Everyone wants this for you.

No one who truly loves you wishes for your pain to continue.

SEE: **MALE GRIEVING SCRIPTS**

TO BE GOOD AT LIFE
IS TO BE GOOD AT THE HAVING AND HOLDING
AND THE LETTING GO...

Peter McGugan

Graduation

The last day of school, few people feel fully prepared to begin selling what they know. There is always doubt, fear and loss involved. There can be grieving. The campus forms a comfortable and familiar womb with a rhythmic pace students understand. For some, graduating is a violent birth.

Build From The Following:

- Finding a job is already your 9 to 5 job.
- Research the marketplace. Identify your passions and goals.
- Attend monthly meetings and conventions of professional associations. They usually have student memberships. Offer to volunteer for the association in exchange for membership or convention enrollment.
- Socialize with people already doing the work you want to do. Take them to lunch and ask for names you might contact.
- Read industry journals and newsletters given to you by your new association contacts.
- Write articles for association newsletters and journals about cutting-edge technology or new developments.
- Become an expert in something. All industries have problems. Find out what they are. Research, read, interview and position yourself as the solution.

SEE: **ZERO ZONE**

When Something Changes Everything

Grief Primer

Grief is not weakness or loss of faith; it is the echoing of love.

- Grief is primal, emotional, illogical, distorting, spiritual, oceanic and uncontrollable. Because you are out of control does not mean you are going crazy.

- Trying to control early grieving is like trying to steer a roller coaster. Just surrender to the pull of your emotions and ride it out.

- You are medically vulnerable. Your immune system is suppressed. Eat a healthy diet; take vitamins. Avoid drugs that retard emotions. Grief is a real and powerful force, and it does not preserve well.

- Everyone had a special and unique relationship with the one you've lost. Your grief will be individual and you can't spare anyone theirs. Others will make their choices. You must create your own process instinctively.

- Avoid constantly being strong. Create a personal time and a place for yourself to come unglued each day.

- Don't try to deal with the lost one's belongings during the first acute phase. Allow their new form of being to become an acceptable reality. Then you will be more able to release their physical presence and send forth their belongings with a tolerable level of sadness and a clearer sense of purpose.

Peter McGugan

- Give yourself a lot of permission. Your memory is preoccupied, so write yourself reminder notes. Take everything easy.

- A grieving driver can be as dangerous as a drunk one. Familiar places, songs, look-a-likes, and the sound-proofed solitude of a car make it a mobile grief-nasium.

   Grieving people are statistically at four times the risk of causing accidents, sometimes deadly. Before setting out, ask yourself honestly if families and pedestrians are safe with you behind the wheel.

Calling a friend, taking a cab or a bus, could save a life.

Guilt

When we do not allow another person to own their life and their death, we use guilt to keep ourselves at the center of their drama.

We regret not verbalizing feelings.

Souls linger with loved ones following death. Anything that needs to be said is already known, but saying it out loud can help you.

To resolve this, imagine yourself a broadcaster of thoughts and beam your invitation out to the soul of your loved one. Affirm that you will only speak to beings of Light and that they must go into the Light before you will communicate with them.

Then, when your sixth sense feels they are listening, openly voice what needs to be said.

You may sense their response.

While we are alive, much of our consciousness sleeps; but once returned to our natural state—pure spirit—we have full consciousness and the petty incidences of what other people did or did not do to us are of little consequence.

What matters most is whether you now choose love and forgiveness, not whether they did.

The frustration of angels is that because we cannot see or photograph a loved one's spirit, we doubt they exist. This is a vital lesson of faith, trust and Love.

Learn to trust what your heart knows. Whether a soul is in or out of a body, you can love them and they will know.

Peter McGugan

Half Hearted Living

To Love with half a heart is to:
- - FEEL HALF A FEELING
- - KNOW HALF A FACT
- - LIVE HALF A LIFE

ENDINGS PRECEDE BEGINNINGS

Happiness

Tell me about two people, one who twelve months ago became a paraplegic and the other a person who won a million in the lottery, and you've not said a thing about their happiness.

What happens to us has little to do with our long-term happiness.

Peter McGugan

Having And Losing EXERCISE

Wh=When we invest in one thing, the door to other options is closed.

Having always involves losing, there are always trade-offs.

Make an honest list of the things you lost by having.

parts of yourself (e.g. spontaneity)

_____

_____

contact with people (e.g. relatives, friends)

_____

_____

time for inner awareness (e.g. spirituality)

_____

_____

relaxations (e.g. films, TV)

_____

_____

activities (e.g. hobbies)

_____

_____

What do you need to do to recover the things you would enjoy? Make some dates with living!

➡

"ALL CREATION REQUIRES CHAOS."
PABLO PICASSO

INNOCENCE IS THE PRICE OF WISDOM.
WHATEVER HASN'T KILLED YOU,
FORGED YOUR SOUL STRONGER.

Peter McGugan

Healing

Physical injuries are primarily healed through the subconscious. Emotional injuries heal more consciously. We poke through the ashes of our past, pondering, wandering, wondering, examining the what ifs and if only Id's.

These tormented moments cauterize emotional wounds.

Healing relies on our ability to release, our ability to forgive and time.

SEE: **CRYING REAL TEARS**

Heaven Is A Nice Peace Of Real Estate
A Story

Following the multiple deaths that changed everything in my life, I ached for the souls I loved and missed. The ones who would have comforted me through loss were the ones I'd lost.

A year after impact, the ache remained an anchor chained on my heart. I was stalled.

The extraction of a wisdom tooth was quickly done and I sat up in the chair to be more comfortable.

Then it was as if someone pushed me back. Suddenly I was being sucked up a vacuum tunnel through darkness speckled with starry lights.

I was before three figures.

On a soul level I could feel a warmth and peace and absolute fullness. It was them!

The ache I'd lived with, the hollow tender void and the empty longing were gone.

Wow!

I was with them.

In a wondrous dimension of pure souls.

They looked beautiful, peaceful, knowing and iridescent.

We shared thoughts. I told them how hard it was—they knew. And I knew my sadness caused their sadness.

"We are fine," they said. "Now, you must go back. You be fine."

Peter McGugan

It was a clarity of Love and union and knowing that I had never imagined. Like melting together as Love.

Things began to move, "We are fine; now you be fine."

I was dropping.

"Oh God, no. Please let me stay."

Dropping, sliding.

"No, please—more."

Commotion around me. Gravity. Thick, heavy, watery air and gravity.

I gasped and filled the body I'd returned to.

Voices. Light on my eyelids.

"He's back," a strange voice said.

The room was filled with dental staff, one with a huge syringe. The kind they inject straight into the heart.

"You feeling better now Peter?"

What a complicated question.

I had no answer.

"Peter, you're okay now, aren't you…Peter?"

"Yes."

The room began to clear.

"Boy that was something," someone said as I closed my eyes and folded my arms over my chest.

My eyes filled with tears. Joy, amazement…gratitude.

Thoughts flooded my mind.

They're okay—no they're wonderful! Oh, they're okay, thank you God. They're O.K.

They're amazing! Wow!

➡

When Something Changes Everything

They're home. Mmmmm. What a succulent dimension.

And I'm here. In this heavy, wet gravity, with Earthlings.

I envied them.

I guess I have work to do.

"Are you crying?"—A woman's caring voice. I wasn't alone.

I wiped huge, wet tears away.

There were still three people in the room, staring, waiting for me to say something.

I'm sure I'd seemed like such a normal guy a few months ago, when I'd spoken at their dental convention.

"I...I just had an experience."

"So did we." said the dental surgeon. He asked about my history of allergic reactions, trying to understand.

I answered his questions, " No...No drug allergies." They expected an explanation.

"I lost my family. They died, and I was just...I just saw them. They told me they're fine and that I need to be fine."

Nobody moved. Stunned expressions.

The impact of what I'd just experienced was profound for me. That was clear to everyone.

The dental surgeon curtly said goodbye and with his assistant scurried down the hall.

I laid there another while...limp, discovering I was soaked in my own sweat.

"I've heard of this."

I turned my head to see a young blond woman who hadn't run away.

She looked at me with searching eyes.

I sniffed and wiped my brow with the cloth someone had put there.

"Do you feel better?" She asked, folded her arms over her chest, looked out the window and asked the question again. "Do you feel better, now that you've seen them?"

What do I feel? I wondered.

Her eyes, the cloudy misted eyes of someone grieving, searched my face.

"I didn't want to come back here," I said.

She stayed in the room while I finished pulling myself together.

"Thanks," I said as I began to leave.

Her look told me she wanted more. "It's really, really nice there."

She heard this with her heart and smiled through tear filled eyes.

I've told very few people about this experience.

Publishing it is something I've resisted because it will affect my credibility with some who will write me off as a kook.

We truly believe only what we experience. And whatever labels or explanations you might apply to this event is of no importance to me. For me, it was a profound turning point. I have been happier with their reality and mine since.

➡

When Something Changes Everything

Their place is one of purer consciousness than I have known. It is pure Love and magnificently connected to the consciousness that is the Life plan.

That Love connection is here for us; it permeates all this thick gravity. But we choose to tap into it or into fear.

This is Schoolhouse Earth, a boot camp for souls.

And when the door of death is naturally offered to us, we graduate to a vastly kinder and gentler dimension.

I know this because I stood at its doorstep.

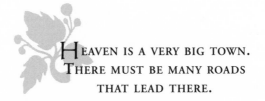

HEAVEN IS A VERY BIG TOWN.
THERE MUST BE MANY ROADS
THAT LEAD THERE.

Peter McGugan

Hidden Emotions

 EXERCISE

Y ou may feel like a mass of contradictory emotions, like a tornado is twisting within you.

It helps to label what you've been feeling.

The inner tornado usually draws strength from a hidden emotion you're afraid to feel.

You may not think relief is what you deserve. You may not have permission from your past to be angry with a lost love, a child, a fallen hero.

Your emotions are all valid and need expression.

Be honest as you feel your layers of emotions and label them here.

- _____
- _____
- _____
- _____
- _____
- _____
- _____
- _____

How can you express the emotions that are hardest for you to feel at peace with?

SEE: ANGER

History Of Loss

EXERCISE

Although this experience feels like no other, you've done it before.

As a child, you released friends, you moved from grade three into grade four. You've released people, pets, infatuations and dreams.

You've trusted life and forgiven.

This time you are not so sure of yourself and the next steps for you. What we're living always feels more intense. Intense means in the present.

Your identity is evolving again and life is telling you to graduate and become something more.

The emptiness you feel must be filled with your own potentials.

This exercise will help you remember the supports, resources and techniques you used to recover from previous losses.

Make a list of previous losses and what helped you get through them.

Loss #1. _____

What got me through was: _____

_____

_____

Loss #2. _____

What got me through was: _____

_____

_____

Peter McGugan

Loss #3. _____

What got me through was: _____

_____

_____

Loss #4. _____

What got me through was: _____

_____

_____

This history of loss offers insights into your recovery strategies and what you may need more of now.

If the one you've lost now got you through before, it is time to expand your boundaries and create new supports. For example, if your spouse always got you through and now he or she is gone, you might find a grief support group.

We each must learn to parent ourselves. Resist this and you feel like a punished, insecure child, and that invites abusive people to use you.

Holding On   🖉EXERCISE

I want you to make a tight fist with one of your hands. Squeeze the fist tightly.

Now, think of what or who you are holding onto.

Keep that fist squeezed tightly, imagine that what you are holding onto is inside.

———•———

How does holding on feel?

Eventually, when you can't hold on any longer, begin to relax your fist back into an open hand and as you do, say, "I'm letting go."

———•———

Do you feel the stranglehold on your heart relax? Does letting go feel better than holding on?

———•———

Letting go requires courage or exhaustion. The choice is yours.

Do this exercise whenever you feel strangled by your stranglehold on the past. Hanging on compounds loss.

Peter McGugan

Hope: A Story

I went in search of a dog. Not wanting to go through the peeing, chewing puppy stages, I asked if the breeder had an older dog. He did. She lived in a cage in a dark spare bedroom at the end of the hall.

"She's no good to me because she won't deliver pups," he explained. "She'll breed, but she won't deliver them. She's a people dog and was used to living with the woman that showed her before I got her. Quite a waste. She was third American champion when she was young."

A metal grooming table stood in the middle of his kitchen. He returned with a bail of smelly knotted Rastafarian hair that showed no sign of head nor tail.

I looked at this canine Cousin It; and when I reluctantly moved nearer to search for eyes, it leaned into me with all its weight.

If I'd stepped back, she would have fallen to the floor.

"Is it healthy?" I asked.

"Oh yes."

From this abused creature I felt nothing but tenderness. To see if this hairball could walk, I took her outside.

Barely able to see, she followed me; each time I stopped she leaned into my leg with all her weight.

➡

When Something Changes Everything

She couldn't maneuver stairs, so I carried her back inside, and sitting her back on the clipping table, asked how much he wanted for her.

The breeder/abuser watched as she, again, leaned into my body; he saw me support and comfort her.

"She's already yours. I've been waiting for someone to take her. It seemed a shame to destroy a dog that likes people."

Concerned for his reputation, he insisted on shearing her. With each head-to-tail run of the clippers, a swath of this beautifully conformed, forgotten champion, emerged.

Muggins took her place as a beloved family member.

When something changed everything and I found myself alone in that echoing house, Muggins and I, the last surviving family members, grieved through months of impossible days and wretched nights.

I'd rescued her, not knowing she would return that favor tenfold.

When I could not stay in that house or that city where everything was laced with memories, I packed my computer, clothes and Muggins into a car and headed out where a loving friend offered refuge.

When my eyes opened each morning, Muggins would nuzzle her head into my neck and give me hope.

Muggins knew all about hope. She'd lived in a small cage at the end of a hall in a room for useless stuff. After living with a woman who'd loved her, made her a champion and then died, Muggins was sold to this breeder.

Peter McGugan

She'd known happiness and love; and for more than two years she waited in that dark cage, only getting out once a day.

During this imprisonment, what went through her mind the morning of day 89?

At 7:30 p.m. on day 632, what kept her believing something better would happen for her? And at 10 a.m. the next morning?

How did she trust that something would change everything?

There was nothing in that two years that she enjoyed, not even the food. Her gums were infected.

What fueled her will to live?

She would emotionally ingest puppies, refusing to bring them into this loveless world. She eliminated their hell, but she did not lose the will to live through her own.

Something in her heart and her spirit knew this would end too. She did not lose heart.

Two years in the dark is a long time to wait for the light. With so much less information, influence or control than you have or I have, she chose hope.

She believed in hoping.

And so can you.

———•——•———

You have a lot more resources to work with, a lot more information.

➡

If a little 15-pound animal can hold on in the dark for two years, you can survive these dark days and nights.

———•———

Muggins was a trooper through the move. After arriving in Dallas, I lived for two years in an office/apartment shared with two other people and a secretary. Muggins and I slept on a mattress in a walk-in closet.

It was our Gandhi phase.

I built a career as a speaker in the U.S., appearing on talk shows and addressing large conventions thinking "If they knew I slept on a closet floor, would they still listen?"

———•———

And gradually I felt alive enough to create a home.

Muggins and I moved to a beautiful house that hangs out over a placid lake. It is surrounded by hills and it nurtures the soul.

It is my well, where I retreat for a fresh cup of life.

Muggins helped me heal.

And then again, she proved her wisdom about change.

At 15, she'd had a couple of little strokes: foreshadowing. She was a bit deaf and had cataracts. In the mornings when she laid her head against my neck, she seemed tired.

Muggins was fading.

Peter McGugan

Then suddenly people commented on how chipper she was, and I'd noticed it too. She was moving with less ache and she could see better. For three days she was bright, agile and very affectionate.

I got home late the third night. "How strange" I thought, "No greeting." Head down, she'd run past me out the front door and into the night.

Usually she gave two barks to let me know she was ready to come in.

Upstairs, in my room, I was overcome with a cold chill of awareness: she's in the lake!

It took me an hour to find her.

She'd dropped herself into the water in a place I'd never known her to go.

When my flashlight revealed her floating body, I heard my shocked self say, "Oh Mugs, look what you've done for me now."

One last gift. A gift of courage and wisdom.

Can a dog be a master of change?

———◆———

Mine was.

H OPE IS A DOOR.
FORGIVENESS IS ITS KEY.

SEE: RESOURCE GUIDE

When Something Changes Everything

Holidays

The holidays are benchmark times when we compare now with before. Celebrations are among the hardest firsts to endure following a loss.

Unfortunately, many people avoid talking about who is missing.

Help them and yourself. Create a special photo album/journal that acknowledges the Christmas history you shared. Fill it with photos, cards, your writing, and commemorate Christmases past.

If you need help, Creative Memories can teach this process. You can find someone in your area who holds workshops by calling (800) 468-9335.

By creating an album, you celebrate the person and traditions and you honor the past. Schedule time to go into the feelings all the way until you and the flood of emotions are exhausted.

Then, compose yourself, gather some adventuresome energy and do the holidays differently. Create new activities.

Holiday Strategies

- Set aside concentrated time to go into and exhaust the feelings. Then you can be with people and celebrate what you have without an accumulation of emotions.

Peter McGugan

- Ask loved ones what doesn't matter. Then do just what matters and create new traditions and sweet spots in time.

- Get active helping the less fortunate. (Believe it or not, there are some.)

- Love, Love, Love the ones you're with.

How Great People Handle Loss
A Story

The most amazing person I've ever met was an 82 year-old woman who lived in Central New Brunswick.

She had been awarded The Order of Canada, the highest national honor, from the prime minister. I was to interview her for television.

My crew and I arrived at her small, white farmhouse set in the middle of a pine forest. I walked into her home and saw an elderly woman with twice as much Life and joy as I.

Her face was beautifully etched by living, and her twinkling eyes are a kaleidoscopic memory. We rocked and talked in front of a crackling wood stove and she told stories of her life.

She had never traveled more than 30 miles from that house. She'd been the self-taught teacher, doctor, mid-wife, and psychic to her 60-mile world. They called her Mother.

She told me stories of life before electricity and telephones, of heading off into a Canadian blizzard to deliver the baby a 'presence' told her was coming.

She spoke of the thirteen children she'd given birth to and the seven that had died. And she remembered the four husbands she loved and lost.

She told the stories of the joys of her life with the same energy she spoke of the tragedies. I asked her why she didn't seem angry or sad when she recalled the horrible things that had happened.

Peter McGugan

She looked right into my eyes and my heart and said, "Every life has joy. Every life has sorrow. I'm not angry to have had mine."

With her own hands she had buried her husbands and more than half of her children. And in the twilight of her life, she spoke of it all, every moment, as a precious and magnificent adventure.

She was right with Life. She forgave Life!

———

The rocking of the boat and the occasional storm are promises of the sea. Nature makes no secret that change, sickness and death are the natural storms of living.

Fate, destiny and Love are the winds in our sails.

When I drove out of that pine forest, my true Life and all the seasons it promised was clearly before me. She revealed life's essential ingredients.

To forgive Life for being so interesting and difficult, so sweetened with joy and bittered with sorrow, so delicious and damned, is perhaps to join the graduating class of Schoolhouse Earth.

When Something Changes Everything

Humor: Losing Your Sense Of It

What are you looking for?

Something I've lost.

Perhaps I can help. What have you lost?

My sense of humor.

Hmmmm. That sounds serious. When did you lose it?

About the time everything changed.

Where had you kept it?

Somewhere in my head. It was like a special pair of lenses that let me see things from interesting angles and perspectives. When I had my sense of humor, I used to be able to see the absurd. Do they still make things absurd?

Yes. Oh yes! All the time. In fact more than ever!

Oh. I haven't seen it in a while…Maybe the absurd is where I left my sense of humor.

Yes. Look for it there.

Peter McGugan

Illness

Loss and unresolved grief weaken our immune response. The year following the death of a spouse we are four times more likely to become seriously ill. We find ourselves flattened by dis-ease, too weak to run.

Illness invites us to heal all parts of our lives. Resistance intensifies pain.

- Become the wise gardener of your Life and consciousness. Where are the weeds that weaken you?

- What doesn't matter? Why do more of it?

- Identify what you can control and what you can't. Build on what you can.

- Allow whatever is happening with your body, priorities and spirit to become the tiller for your new life course.

- This is an invitation to reinvent yourself and your relationships.

- On Schoolhouse Earth we're offered lessons of Loving, Sharing, Faith, Forgiveness and Humility.

Resist—and wellness is impaired. Become a student of the lesson.

Imbalance

Like a jewel, you have many facets. When light entering one facet of a diamond is diminished, all the light within dims.

You are a physical being needing movement; you are a tribal being needing people, a spiritual being, an intellectual being, a sexual being...

Well-being requires balance.

On a scale of 1 to 10, rate these aspects of your life in terms of the fulfillment you derive from them today.

_____ spiritual

_____ social

_____ career/involvements

_____ child self

_____ sexual

_____ financial

Then, with 10 (the outer edge of the wheel) being very fulfilling and 0 (the inner point of the wheel) being very unfulfilling, fill in the slices of the pie as illustrated.

Peter McGugan

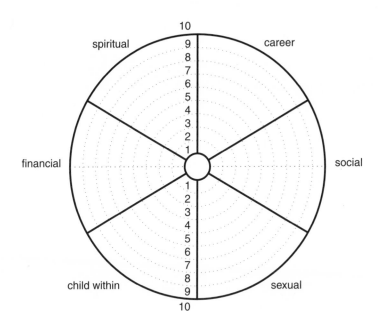

When it is filled in, view it as a wheel. How well rounded is your life? How does your life roll along? Where are you imbalanced? Which facets of yourself need to be fuller?

SEE: **BALANCE AND IMBALANCE**

Impact...The Emotional Swamp

In a moment something changes everything. Impact deals its devastating blow to your consciousness, your spirit and your dreams. The future you anticipated dissolves into a ghostly mist of the mind.

You plunge into the Zero Zone. Shocked, limp and confused, reality's damp chill penetrates you.

Time stalls.

Thoughts cross your mind at warp speed and pathetic crawls. With rapid-fire awareness, you drown in sensations.

Lurching, weeping, wandering, raging, collapsing. These are steps of the grief dance.

Loss devastates identity, self-worth, security, position, home, pummeling every cell of your being.

The journey out of the emotional swamp of overwhelming grief is slow, painful, cold, wet, moment by moment.

The void is vast.

Injured and weak, we begin the journey out of the cold loneliness of the emotional swamp and through the Zero Zone.

To move forward, through this winter of the soul, there must be a reason, an inkling of purpose.

Seek it, pray for it, listen and move toward it.

SEE: **READER PATH: ACCIDENTS AND DISASTERS**

Peter McGugan

Investing

All investment leaves us vulnerable to loss. As we begin to care, to value, to identify our Self with anything or anyone, we are at risk of losing.

The choice is to never invest in anything and never risk the pain of loss, or to fulfill the caring nature of being a spiritual being in a human body and travel the precarious and tender paths of loving, losing and letting go.

There is no choice. Life finds you because you are Life!

To resist caring, and investing in people and situations is passive suicide. It is to kill the kaleidoscope of feelings, experiences and sweet spots in time to avoid risking dark days and nights of the soul.

On any journey, the valleys are rich, dark and thick with nature's entanglements of growth, while nothing grows on the peaks.

We do not grow on life's peaks, we grow in its valleys.

Struggle and pain are our greatest teachers.

TRAGEDY IS
THE SHROUD OF MIRACLES.

Jealousy

Like an emotional cancer, jealousy consumes a soul. It feeds on itself while the good, loving, happy, confident and forgiving person is eaten away.

The jealous person becomes the victimized, wronged estranged one who does not let go.

Jealousy's choking grip cannot hold a person who takes a step into a new future.

Find a purpose for yourself and leave the past where it wants to be...behind you. Get something new happening.

The jealous person seeks blame and evil in others, when in truth, darkness—the seed of which may have been in the perpetrator—now grows as a thorny weed within the jealous one.

Jealousy consumes wisdom to keep its ugly self alive. Knowing it cannot last where there is forgiveness, faith, or forward movement, dark jealousy prods you to hurt and destroy so your choices will be taken away.

Jails are filled with people who did not move toward a new future. They gave jealousy control and are now jealous of everyone in the free world.

Among criminals jealousy won.

If jealousy is consuming you, get help from a support group, a therapist or a wise friend.

Do not follow jealousy's thoughts; they'll lead you on a path to hell.

Peter McGugan

Journaling

Journaling moves what's on your mind off of your mind.

Thoughts are things. Paper is a good place to store the troubling ones.

Buy yourself a notebook and start writing.

Feelings are thoughts in motion. Your journal gives them a safe place to land.

SEE: **OBSESSING**

Joy

TIME IS PATIENT.
JOY AND HAPPINESS ARE NOT.
WHEN YOU REFUSE THEM, THEY ARE GONE.

WOULD THE ONE YOU'VE LOST
WANT TO HAVE STOLEN JOY FROM YOU?

WHO WINS WHEN YOU REFUSE JOY?

Peter McGugan

Living In Your Body

We give house tours saying, "And this is the room we live in."

We also live in parts of our being. Some people live in their stomach and exist for food. Others live in their analytical mind and intellectualize their life experience. Some live in their sexuality. Others live in their wallet and bank account, believing life is about their stuff.

Wherever you lived, loss plunged you into your heart.

This can be terrifying.

As we cross the Zero Zone, we experience the vast horizons of the heart. We learn to survive there.

We are born living in our hearts. We enter Life as love and loss initiates a conscious return to Love.

SEE: **LOVE, LOVE AND LUV**

Loss And Gains EXERCISE

With loss there is gain. Independence, spontaneity, options, closet space!

Many of us feel guilty for taking any pleasure in the gains of loss.

Imagine the situation being reversed. If you were on the *other side of the fence,* would you want people to stay closed and guilty?

Who wins by your not enjoying the gains?

The Gain Exercise
Make a list of all the things you've gained.

- _____
- _____
- _____
- _____
- _____
- _____
- _____
- _____
- _____
- _____
- _____
- _____

Peter McGugan

Refusing to enjoy the gains of your loss is committing to blame. We blame everyone else, ourselves, them, God and Life, refusing to learn the lessons and participate in our own potentials.

Staying in blame compounds your loss.

Outline a plan to cultivate the four most important things on your gains list.

Gain #1. _____

I can enjoy this more by:_____

_____

_____

Gain #2. _____

I can enjoy this more by:_____

_____

_____

Gain #3. _____

I can enjoy this more by:_____

_____

_____

Gain #4. _____

I can enjoy this more by:_____

_____

_____

Schedule dates and times to develop and enjoy each gain without guilt. Grieving is difficult, courageous work. You've earned pleasure.

When Something Changes Everything

Love, love And Luv

Love

Capital L, Love is what we long for. It is the nurtured connection that says I will love you more tomorrow than I do today. And with time, the roots of our relationship will grow deeper, stronger.

love

Small l love is very common. It grows from loneliness and compatibility rather than commitment. Its premise: I love you and I'll always love you until I don't any more.

We yearn for Love. What we bring home is too often love.

Luv

As in *Luv ya baby.*

With the depth of a puddle, it's too much, too soon and over too fast.

Luvers flit from scene to scene, using luv to get attention and sex, running red hot then ice cold.

Luvers are the casualties of Hollywood.

SEE: THIRD ENERGY, REBOUNDS,
SNAKES IN THE BRAIN,
SEXUAL 911

Peter McGugan

Love Over Fear

We do not fear our own weakness. What we fear and resist is our own greatness.

You are composed of potentials, but most people fear and sabotage the gifts they're alive to share.

There are two ways to get attention: being weaker or stronger or being very bad or very good.

You choose to be wonderful or pitiful.

The attention we get for being very bad is short lived and quickly turns toxic.

Everything happens to everyone in one form or another. It's not what happens to you, it's what you do with it.

When you need to grieve, overflow with it.

Then it will be time to lift and apply yourself to living something worthwhile.

The angels wait for you to recognize and release the greatness and potentials you contain.

SEE: **BE THE GIFT**

When Something Changes Everything

Male Grieving Scripts

Grief is an intimate process. A waltz with your soul. Our culture has licensed women to be more emotionally expressive than men.

But it isn't just social. Women have a hormone called prolactin that encourages crying and tears. Male hormones can retard the crying process.

Men can comfortably release panic in *safe* masculine ways like whacking baseballs, golf balls, chopping wood, lifting weights, getting drunk or picking a fight.

Historically, men have been taught to grieve by smashing or getting smashed. Leading men haven't done the wailing or weeping scenes.

Most women are more open with their emotions, except those who were raised in a Victorian manner of grieving. Queen Victoria taught us to grieve by swallowing it and wearing black forever...that was it!

We were all supposed to *take it like a man.*

During the Victorian Era rashes, asthma and other psychogenic symptoms of repressed emotions flourished and "band-aid medicine" as we still know it, flourished by creating drugs to erase the surface symptoms of repressed emotions.

No life is without seasons of agonizing loss. Your relationship with who and what you've lost was personal and unique and your recovery will be as unique.

Talk about what you are feeling, grieving and missing and allow yourself and others to 'lose control.'

Peter McGugan

Don't be saying, "Don't cry, don't worry." It is better to say, "Have a big cry, let your feelings out," and then let it flow.

We must not judge the way another person endures their loss. Grief is the most intimate experience we have with ourselves.

What we need during these times is love, acceptance and the ability to choose the people we communicate with.

SEE: **DIFFERENCES IN GRIEVING, MEN AND CRYING**

Media

Scandals and crises grip our televisions and homes. Frantic barrages of sensational gossip, propaganda and magnified misinformation are splashed across the screens and straight into our minds and hearts.

As crises or wars unfold, we absorb the controlled hysteria of a media as anxious to be first as to be accurate.

And, like deer hypnotized by thought-numbing headlights, we are frozen in front of the screen, magnifying the impact of the crime just by being there to absorb it into our fertile consciousness.

When something is changing everything in your life, consider taking yourself on a negativity fast. Avoid all disruptive unreliable influences.

The popular media can be carcinogenic to peace of mind.

SEE: SCANDAL

Peter McGugan

Men And Crying

Being strong for everyone else doesn't work. It puts your health and heart at risk. It alienates you from the powerful process your mind, spirit and body need to be doing—crumbling and then rebuilding.

Denying grief makes you an emotional zombie. You are a spiritual being having a human experience. Your spirit's feelings need expression.

Unfortunately boys are programmed not to cry. We lose permission to purge ourselves in the most natural and effective way. This is a great human tragedy. Stagnant tears age into rage.

Unexpressed emotions lead men to bizarre forms of violence, abuse, addictions and despair.

Crying is our healthiest way of releasing pain. We know this; but even as an emotional trigger fires off a charge of emotion, crying can feel childish and indulgent.

The truth is, healthy men cry. Frightened men do not.

When a powerful flood of emotion hits your face and eyes, let it flow or quickly find a safe place for yourself and release it, rather than tensing your face and throat and stuffing it back down inside your body.

Tears of joy and sorrow are the bloodstream of loving. To deny them is tragic isolation from your life's most important moments.

When you refuse to cry out for love, you deny yourself the sweetest, most tender truth.

Regardless of everything you've been taught, your soul is Love.

Misery

MISERY IS BEAUTIFUL
IN THE LATE AFTERNOON
WHEN EVERYTHING SHADES ROSE
AND THE WORLD REFLECTS ENDINGS AND
SADNESS.
I WONDER,
WANDER,
PONDER.
I TRULY LOVED
WITH ALL MY HEART
WHAT I HAVE LOST.

SEE: **LOVE OVER FEAR**

Peter McGugan

Mother Symbiosis

MOTHER.
YOU WERE THE FAUCET,
I WAS THE CUP.
YOU WERE AN OCEAN,
I THE SPONGE.
YOU SYMBIOTICALLY SUCKLED ME INTO LIFE,
THEN PUSHED ME OFF THE BREAST
SO THAT I WOULD WALK.
AND SO I WALK
THROUGH CHANGE AFTER CHANGE,
CHAPTER AFTER CHAPTER,
CREATING BREASTS
TO DRINK THEM DRY.
A CONSUMER OF EXPERIENCE, I WALK ON AND ON
SEEKING THE NEXT BREAST
AND THE NEXT.
THAT DELICIOUS SYMBIOSIS,
WAS IT REAL?
I MAY BE IN THIS WORLD
BUT I'M NOT REALLY OF THIS WORLD.

Mama told us nothing bad
was ever going to happen to us.
Storybooks said, "They lived happily ever after."

Nobody told us the honest truth.

We gather, have and hold
and then release everything...
piece by piece.

It helps to know.

Peter McGugan

Moving

We hard-wire ourselves into people and places.
Moving demands that we cut a thousand connections.
There is grieving, longing, frustration.
Gradually we wire ourselves into the new place.
Friendships grow through laughter, time and adversity. We have to mix with many people before we find the chemistry of friendship.
To wire yourself into your new place more quickly:

- Become a student of the new region. Using tourism brochures, create your own orientation program and schedule events on the calender.

- Invite locals to see the local attractions they've never seen.

- When one note on a piano is struck, the same note on any nearby piano responds. You'll hit a few sour notes before finding people that respond to you with friendship. Be true to your note.

- Interested people are interesting. Learn as much as you can about where you are from people already there.

- Join spiritual organizations, clubs and associations that interest you. Take some night classes.

- Ask people about the best fund raising and charity events. Make a donation, and you'll get invitations galore!

- Customs, cultures, values, terminology, trust levels and sincerity differ by city and region. As a student of a new culture, be easy on yourself and the many people who disappoint you.

When Something Changes Everything

Negativity Fast EXERCISE

On the left side below, list what gives you pleasure and joy. Don't censor or edit. Include things like seeing different things, music, fun, positive thoughts, hobbies and things you would like to do. Just let your hand do the writing.

Go ahead and don't hold back.

pleasure	pain
_____	_____
_____	_____
_____	_____
_____	_____
_____	_____
_____	_____
_____	_____
_____	_____
_____	_____
_____	_____
_____	_____
_____	_____
_____	_____
_____	_____

Once you've filled the left side, fill the right side with things that don't make you feel good. Think of habits, memories, mementos, photos, people, diversions. Be honest. Just let it flow.

Peter McGugan

How can you be with the pleasurable things more and the painful ones less?

Go through each one and create a plan for having more pleasure and less pain.

Pain is not about the past as much as the present and what you refuse to release.

Letting go of some anchors to the past is a necessary passage.

What needs to go into the closet? What needs to go out the door?

You have permission to be a wonderful and happy person.

WHENEVER I THOUGHT ABOUT IT,
I FELT ILL.
AND SO, AT LONG LAST,
I CAME TO A BRILLIANT DECISION.
I DECIDED NOT TO THINK ABOUT IT.

When Something Changes Everything

Nighttime: Slaying The Dragons

As if the days aren't exhausting enough, you lie awake, buzzing with the excruciating realities you most need to escape.

You need a break; but your mind whirls into the night sorting through your mental pantry of memories, expectations and dreams.

In the quiet of night, naked with the truth, we clean our emotional and spiritual house.

These are the hardest and most important times of grieving.

Emotions do only two things: they get buried within and fester or they flow outward and evaporate.

Let feelings flow.

SEE: DRUGS, POSITIVE THINKING CAP

Peter McGugan

Obsessing

Unbridled obsessing mounts up to create a future-damning litany of thoughts, memories and emotions that compound on themselves. It is a mental lock on dead options, confused communications, regretful occurrences and moments of the mist that are all rooted in regret.

Whatever you think about expands.

When today doesn't perform well on the stage of your mind, yesterdays take center stage.

If you are not yet sick and tired of feeling sick and tired, your obsessing may still be healthy. It's the trials in your mind, deliberation on who is guilty and innocent. (See "trials in your mind.")

To exhaust obsessive thoughts that just won't quit, seek out the lesson that is to be learned from the experience. Behind each obsessive thought is an occurrence and within each occurrence, a lesson.

Obsessing Exercise #1

1. To do this take a piece of paper and describe, in minute detail, each event you obsess about.

2. After writing a really honest description of the event, outline the first time and other times you recall having these feelings. Look for the patterns. Are there themes throughout your losses?

➡

Ask your inner wisdom and another wise person what the lesson, or choice of the highest good (the win/win/win for all), may be in this situation.

If the highest good means you would make the same choices, it is done. Let it go by disposing of your transcript.

If the highest good is to do it differently, write the better choice down. Absorb this lesson into all parts of your being. Affirm, write, meditate, sing and chant this lesson, this choice you are incorporating and will make in the future. Stay with this until you are completely bored with it.

When we learn a lesson, obsessions stop chasing us and we open ourselves to the opportunities of now and what's next.

Obsessing Exercise #2: Surrender And Celebration

When you are tired and bored with your obsessive self it is time to refocus.

When you pull yourself together and fix your story, you have the strength to nurture and celebrate your potentials instead of your imperfect past.

For two days, promise yourself that whenever you have an obsessive thought you will look at and act on the surrender and celebration list you've created on the following page. Focus and act on what you've got to celebrate and you will wrestle control of your mind and the thoughts it presents. The downward, ever darkening spiral of obsessions will slow, stop and reverse direction. By gaining control you align your mind with fixing your story.

This is intense, moment-to-moment work recommended only after you are exhausted with your own obsessing.

This exercise pays off with the sweetest lessons and rewards.

Surrender And Celebration

What in your life deserves to be celebrated?

1._____

2._____

3._____

4._____

5._____

6._____

7._____

What needs to be surrendered?

1._____

2._____

3._____

4._____

5._____

6._____

7._____

After two days of really focusing on celebrating and building on what you have, decide whether obsessing is better than celebrating.

SEE: **SURRENDERING, TRIALS IN YOUR MIND**

When Something Changes Everything

Opening

Something changed everything.
You changed too.
There is no choice, you've already done it.
All that is left is surrender.
Resistance is the root of pain, and no one wants agony for you.
Try opening your mind, your heart, your arms and your Life to receive what is next.
Do this with me.
As you spread your arms wide open say, "I'm open to what is next for me."
Try this now.

How did that feel?
Is there resistance?
Do it again and again, each time with more conviction. You will feel the straightjacket of resistance loosen.
By affirming what you want, you'll be teaching all parts of yourself to follow your conscious wishes.
Try this as a daily morning exercise and see how much more the day offers when you open to receive.

Peter McGugan

Pain: The Path Out Of Misery

We need to go through the pain, remembering, feeling, retching and releasing. Better to have the stabs now than to ignore this new truth and allow the feelings, thoughts and emotions to fester and surface as ugly mutations later.

TO BE EXCELLENT AT LIFE
DOESN'T MEAN NOT HAVING PAIN.
IT MEANS USING PAIN
TO BE EXCELLENT AT LIFE.

When Something Changes Everything

Parent Loss

When a parent dies, we feel ripped from our safe moorings.

We drift.

Our anchor is gone. We become adult orphans.

We grieve them, ourselves, the generations here and yet to arrive as we witness time's human tide.

Generations wash ashore on Schoolhouse Earth to learn, laugh, live and love. And then they graduate.

This is the divine Life plan your parents were instruments of.

So…learn, live, love and laugh some more.

This is what loving parents wish for their children.

LET NO PART OF YOU DIE WITH ME MY CHILD
FOR I BLOOM AGAIN WITHIN YOU.
GATHER ALL THE GOODNESS AND STRENGTHS
THAT I AM WITHIN YOU,
AND LIVE THEM, BE THEM, TEACH THEM.
AND THROUGH YOU, WITH YOU,
I AM.

Peter McGugan

Moments On The Journey Of Parent Loss

You reach for the phone to call and realize they are not there.

Were you calling for them or for yourself? What are you needing—reassurance, comforting, parenting?

What other options do you have?

What person would your parent be pleased for you to talk to now?

How can you parent yourself today?

Is there an older person who is parental toward you? Can you spend time with them? They may appreciate you as much as you appreciate them.

After a parent's death, siblings are volatile. They may revert to childish behavior—perhaps thinking the parent will reappear to reprimand. The loss can make siblings selfish and greedy, confusing the parent's stuff with the parent.

People grieve in strange and amazing ways and settling the estate can bring out the best or worst in people.

Parents need to make their wishes very, very clear. But when there are no clear instructions, find a mediator to help resolve things.

The stuff won't fix the hurt.

Some clichés are powerful.

YOU DON'T KNOW WHAT YOU HAVE TILL IT'S GONE.

➡

The twisted path of blaming punishing and criticizing yourself for what you didn't do when you could have is a natural part of recovery.

It's best if you walk through it quickly.

When do we do enough loving? When do we spend enough time?

When I speak, I'll often ask, "When have you done enough parenting?" And the overwhelming answer is "Never."

When have you done enough for your parents?

If the scale is very imbalanced, then do something now.

- Plant a garden in their honor.

- Make a list of the qualities they taught you and become them more.

- Make a list of other ways you can honor who they were.

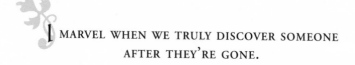

I MARVEL WHEN WE TRULY DISCOVER SOMEONE AFTER THEY'RE GONE.

SEE: READER PATH: LOSS OF A PARENT

Peter McGugan

Partners: When You Lose Your Partner

Partnerships work because of a division of responsibilities.

While stunned by loss, our abilities to learn, to deal with bills, mortgages, plumbing, grass cutting, auto insurance, lawyers, debts, leaky roofs and estates are diminished. Attention spans shrink.

Panic is not a good state in which to learn new skills or recover rusty ones.

Here are some steps to consider.

1. Assume responsibility for your business decisions.

2. Ask for reliable, trustworthy, affordable guidance and advice.

3. Always get two opinions.

4. When you are ready, take courses, read books, know what's up.

5. Always get second opinions before deciding.

6. Always compare prices.

7. Mind your own business.

SEE: ANGER, HOLDING ON, THIRD ENERGY, HOW GREAT PEOPLE HANDLE LOSS, FRIENDS

People At Work

I f you have a physical injury, you are hospitalized. Friends bring flowers, relatives send cards, you stay in bed. You get pampered.

Battered by hurricane force winds of change, the emotionally injured are not admitted for round-the-clock care.

We are expected to show up for work, do the job, be efficient and rejoin our materialistic culture, which doesn't make sense any more.

People at work need to know you're going through a dramatic change.

The following is something I've written for you to photocopy and give them:

Peter McGugan

Dear_____:

Sometime in your life something changed everything. If you remember how grief paralyzes time, you will begin to understand where I am now.

I'd like to be better, I'd like to be my normal self again. I'd like that very much.

But I'm not myself. I'm healing and recreating myself and that takes time.

I am not a machine that breaks down and gets fixed over the weekend. People don't heal that way so please treat me like a person, not a machine.

If you can be caring, compassionate and supportive, I will recover more quickly.

You have my permission to jolt me back to reality, but please do it gently because I'm going through something big.

I thank you so very much for your caring and patience.

Change happens to everyone; and if you'll help me through this, I'll be equipped to help when something changes everything in your life.

No, I'm not Okay yet, but I'm working on it.

When Something Changes Everything

Perfection

W e've all suffered an imperfect past. Life has not turned out the way any of us expected it to, and contained within this tumultuous ride is Life's divine bitter sweet perfection.

Doing this exercise will help you heal your relationship with change.

Think of a perfect moment in time. Imagine this as fully as you can and then freeze it.

———◆———

How long were you there before you got bored and edgy and needed something to change, something to do?

Change is the bloodstream of living.

While we fear and resent its force on our lives, we also need it.

Without change, consciousness only sleeps.

Peter McGugan

Phobias And Panic

Fear takes on a life of its own. It is the flip side of faith.

A frightened mind exaggerates a mouse into a shadowy monster that chases and corners us.

Knowledge is toxic to fear. Examination shrinks phobias.

Focus on what you can control and from there begin exploring, learning, and probing. A library is a wonderful place to shrink fears with knowledge.

To be free of phobias, awake each day and ask, "What am I afraid of today?" Then take baby steps toward it.

Approach fears with wisdom, guidance and knowledge. If you do this, you will be truly free and empowered.

Neuro Linguistic Programming (NLP) is the most effective method of overcoming phobias.

SEE: **HOLDING ON**

Positive Thinking Cap   ✐ EXERCISE

On a sleepless and very lonely night I prayed for help. My eyes settled on a cap tossed on the dresser. I affirmed fifty times that while wearing it, only positive thoughts of the future would fill my mind.

Think your way through the floods of inner thoughts, the "what ifs, if only I'ds" and "maybe ifs," until you are exhausted, then allow your positive thinking cap to navigate you into the future.

Empower it as protection against obsessing and use it in good mental health

SEE: **NIGHTTIME: SLAYING THE DRAGONS, OBSESSING**

Peter McGugan

Prayer

The power of prayer will continue to amaze science and medicine because it cannot be dissected under a microscope or cultured in a petri dish.

The soul is its witness.

Focused thought has the power to alter conditions, heal relationships and people. Prayer has been proven to transcend time and space again and again.

Prayer works.

For further insights, find Larry Dossey's book *Power of Prayer* in your library or book store.

To generate a prayer alliance, Unity churches hold 24-hour prayer vigils. You can create one by calling (800) 669-7729.

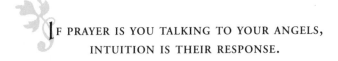

IF PRAYER IS YOU TALKING TO YOUR ANGELS,
INTUITION IS THEIR RESPONSE.

Public Relations

We the grieving are not well people. Let's admit it. We can't fake being happy or efficient without damaging ourselves even more.

Saying "I'm okay" when you're not okay is lying about your truth. It isolates you from recovery, from yourself and from people who care.

Recovery takes years, not weeks, so resist becoming your own spin doctor.

Each morning sense how you really are. Admit, "I'm fragile today" and let caring people care.

Where you are on the path of recovery is where you need to be today. Rush and you'll stumble.

Recovery is one moment, one awareness, one step, one day at a time.

SEE: QUICK FIXES, STAGES OF GRIEF

Peter McGugan

Questions

THERE ARE ONLY SIX GREAT QUESTIONS.

OF WHAT IS YOUR SPIRIT COMPOSED?

WHAT FORMS RELATIONSHIPS?

WHAT IS SACRED?

WHAT IS BORN FROM PAIN?

WHAT IS WORTH DYING FOR?

WHAT IS WORTH LIVING FOR?

THE ANSWER:

LOVE

When Something Changes Everything

Quick Fixes

We love machines. They break today and are fixed tomorrow. But you are not a machine.

There are no real shortcuts to recovery.

We may fake a recovery, burying ourselves in work, busyness, becoming frantic doers lurching back into the fast lanes too tender, too soon.

Those who detour the Zero Zone have not recovered. They wear the brittle armor of the walking wounded. They go, go, go, afraid to stop long enough to feel. They burn out.

As much as we would like a Hollywood movie life, it cannot be.

We cannot cut to a commercial and then come back to a scene of blissful recovery in which the lost pieces have been replaced. That's not Life; that's the lie Hollywood tells us.

Life takes time, tears and forgiveness to heal.

Because your mourning goes on and on does not mean you are crazy or failing...it simply means you're feeling. And that is good. Feelings are the path out of the darkness of loss.

Peter McGugan

Rage And I

I HAVE A NEW COMPANION.
RAGE.
THIS NEW COMPANION SWEEPS ME INTO ITS CLUTCH AND
SQUEEZES GOODNESS AWAY.
I DON'T LIKE THE PLACES RAGE LEADS ME.
I THINK IT'S TIME FOR ME TO DUMP RAGE.
THIS RELATIONSHIP HAS TO END TOO.

When Something Changes Everything

Re-entry

My re-entry is to write this book for us.

What can you do with your time?

Can you create something with it? Can you make a quilt, write poetry, join an association, volunteer, find old friends, take a trip, send a lot of letters?

It isn't vital that you do something creative; but at the very least, spend some time with children.

Peter McGugan

Rebounds

Finally I've found you.
The one.
We're going to be wonderful together.
I had to get dumped
to find you!
I had to go through this!
I understand everything now!
What did you say your name was?

Loved ones fill your heart's inner spaces. No matter the
time or distance, the Soul/Love occupies their unique
space in your heart. They are not replaced.

When someone we love is gone, our heart must heal;
it must reshape itself.

The seasons of the heart work much like a garden.

But spring-summer, spring-summer, spring-summer,
leads us to collapse. We must endure the cold winters
of the soul.

Your heart must be well enough to offer a healthy
space for a lover to solidly occupy. Broken hearts can't
contain a relationship.

The season must be right for blooming.

SEE: LOVE, LOVE, LUV,
SNAKES IN THE BRAIN,
SEXUAL 911

Recovery

Recovery is a lofty clearing from which we look back and say, "It happened. It's okay that it happened. I'm okay now."

You arrive there after wading through the emotional swamps, crossing the Zero Zone and climbing the unexplored horizon of your next future.

It begins by slowly feeling your way out of the darkness. It is not smooth or gradual. Recovery is more like this:

Peter McGugan

Releasing

Every one and everything we have, we release. That is the life process.

You've been doing this all along, moving from grade three to grade four, moving through relationships.

Do you remember how much you loved your first car? Do you remember how protective you were of it? Where is that car now? For that matter, where is your very first love?

Life is the process of attracting, having, holding and releasing.

HOLD WHAT YOU HAVE,
ATTRACT WHAT YOU NEED,
AND RELAX YOUR GRIP
ON WHAT IS GONE.

When Something Changes Everything

Resistance

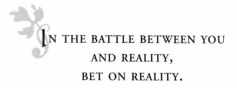

IN THE BATTLE BETWEEN YOU
AND REALITY,
BET ON REALITY.

SEE: SURRENDERING

Peter McGugan

Reverse The Situation   🖉 EXERCISE

I f a loved one died and you are stuck between this world and the one they're in, do the following.

Imagine yourself being a spirit...able to observe your loved ones.

You are the angel. What would you be encouraging them to do?

If you saw them doing what you've been doing, what would you want to communicate to them?

Refusing Life, when we are alive, makes angels cry.

The following questions will lead you to important answers.

What would you wish for people who love you if you were the one in spirit form?

What do your angels wish for you?

What do you wish for yourself?

If you deny goodness, laughter and your future potentials, who wins?

When Something Changes Everything

Scandal

We imagine it will follow us everywhere, always. Scandal, acrid as the smell of burning flesh, taints even the air we breath.

If scandal is burning through your life, remember how soon its audiences forget. Tomorrow's story sends the scandal chasers scurrying to another home.

Memories and judgments fade until all that remains is scandal's sediment—the slight thrill of proximity.

All scandals mellow.

When the media/wolf is at your door, take yourself on a negativity fast. Protect your mind and faith by accepting information only from trusted insiders.

Focus on loving and supporting the other people affected and get them on the negativity fast.

Most scandals burn hot and fast, and we never know how it will end until the ride is over.

It does end. Hang on.

Grocers would not feature rotten food, but they are shameless vendors of rotten journalism when they put tabloids at eye-level in the checkout aisles.

These septic tanks of thought plaster headlines that—whether we buy them or not—contaminate the consciousness of child and parent.

Ultimately what society's perpetually ignorant think of your story is really none of your business.

SEE: **NEGATIVITY FAST**

Peter McGugan

Safety is a paper house illusion.
Be willing to step outside
to risk the elements of change,
to BE.
Staying safe inside isn't safety,
it is suicide.

When Something Changes Everything

Scarcity Is A Lie

When you want the same piece of cake you've just eaten, how can you have it?

And could it be as good the second time you ate it?

There is no shortage of whatever you have lost unless you insist it be the same as it was before.

The supply of what you've had never dries up as long as you're open to another season, anew.

Peter McGugan

Separation And Divorce

Relationships are electric.

They have the most refined voltage and flow we can perceive. They exist on a mutually sustained charge.

When a relationship is dying we're tempted to believe someone is its murderer. If we stalk the killer, lay blame and seek revenge, it becomes a massacre.

Separation is more confusing than loss.

Hard-wired into the relationship, the physical, emotional, mental and spiritual circuits are still charged up, regardless of the distance between the people.

When one partner disconnects, the relationship's current of Love, need and desire short circuits, smokes, sparks, ignites, flames, burns and smoulders.

Regardless of the geographical distance, we feel disconnection and internally sort out the radical flow—the backwash of our own love.

Each of a thousand fine and delicate connections must be cut before we are self-generated and free again.

As the fuses blow and circuits short, you are confused, irrational and scattered. The spinning whirlwind of Love, hate, grief, confusion and hope flips you inside out.

Separating is emotional cerebral palsy.

Your tenderest fears about abandonment, self-worth, attractiveness, age, potentials, financial security that were soothed and lulled into a deep sleep awaken in a growling toxic fury.

Each new day apart earns us the wretched blessing of time and distance. With enough of both, the magnetics and chemistry are inert. And the pain subsides.

➡

When Something Changes Everything

A Separation Action Plan

- Think clearly and act calmly. Consult people before acting on your cauldron of boiling emotions.

- Concentrate on building your spiritual, physical, mental and financial self-confidence.

- Be honest about the players in your life drama. Do you rerun the same fiction again and again?

- In many tribes the wounded lover is taken away by caring confidants and comforted, consoled, bolstered and renewed before returning to the tribe. Is there a quiet, safe place you can get away to? Nature is a healing companion.

- Research indicates that trying to put your Ex out of your mind doesn't work. Talk about them, think and write in your journal, join a support group and let thoughts and feelings flow until you are exhausted.

- If you are locked into an obsession, seek an experienced therapist or ask to be referred to a recovery group.

- If you have children, Parents Without Partners has more than 800 groups in the U.S. They provide support, information and social activities. Call (800) 637-7974 or (301) 588-9354. The address is 8807 Colesville Road, Silver Springs, MD 20910.

SEE: **READER PATH: SEPARATION, DIVORCE, LOSS OF A LOVE, RESOURCE GUIDE, ANGER, LONELINESS, SNAKES IN THE BRAIN, SEXUAL 911, REBOUNDS, OBSESSING**

Peter McGugan

Sexual 911

The mortality rate among uncuddled babies is extremely high. We need touch. Sexual 911 is a stopgap on our frightened flight from separateness.

If intimacy is what you think you need, be smart...be safe and be realistic. We long to instantly recover what we once had, the lost lover, deliverer of bliss.

Other people do not give you the feelings and emotions you experience. You give yourself happiness when the clauses of your personal happiness contract are satisfied.

Your best option is a good professional massage. It satisfies the hunger for touch.

SEE: **THIRD ENERGY, REBOUNDS, SNAKES IN THE BRAIN**

DON'T SEND ME SOMEONE WONDERFUL.
HELP ME DISCOVER I'M SOMEONE WONDERFUL.

Shopping In The Zero Zone

In our quest to feel full again, we risk foolishness. Change is necessary, but surrounding yourself with new stuff will not erase the emptiness that follows heartfelt loss.

If you've yearned for something and can afford it, decide slowly.

Big decisions deserve the guidance of three knowing friends.

SEE: ZERO ZONE

Peter McGugan

Sleep Programming

Several sleepless nights is natural following an emotional earthquake. As the impact settles on your mind, your consciousness whirs.

It is exhausting.

It is important to be programming yourself for good sleep. Try this type of programming:

I will sleep peacefully through the night.
I am safe and protected.
I will awaken in the morning
feeling light and refreshed.

Make a little hum or song and repeat this information twenty times as you are getting ready for bed.

Chanting is the most effective, natural way of self-programming. It's telling your mind what you want so it can deliver.

As you fall asleep, you can program yourself for what you will dream, who you will be with in your dreams, whether you will remember your dream, what creative answers you will awaken with, and the type of day you'll have tomorrow. Tell yourself how you want to feel. Chant your desires.

Take charge of what you want your mind to be doing.

SEE: POSITIVE THINKING CAP

When Something Changes Everything

Snakes In The Brain

We each have snakes in the brain—serpent thoughts we feed, fear or overcome.

What are the things you honestly expect from relationships?

To really benefit, write them down now.

We run scripted patterns in our relationships and these scripts are played out again and again.

Love, and the hunger for it is blinding.

We tend to see what we want to see, so wake up and be honest about your relationship scripts.

Are your expectations realistic? Can anyone deliver?

What do you need to change about these scripts?

Is there anything you've expected a lover to deliver that only you can do for yourself?

Making these changes successfully is overcoming the snakes in your brain.

Relationship Scripts

Lovers reveal their relationship scripts and how they'll treat you, often on the second or third date. When we describe the patterns of past relationships, we're describing how we expect relationships to unfold.

Hearing it on the first date is a red flag; they are in too big a hurry, writing their contract too soon. It'll probably be a one-act play.

Peter McGugan

In the future, listen very carefully when people describe past relationships, marriages and affairs. Listen as they describe your role. Ask questions.

Unless the person is getter smarter or is working hard to change the patterns and scripts and kill the serpents, you are being auditioned for a leading role in the same old play.

It has to get bad enough for people to change and make themselves better. Unless it's gotten really bad or they've gotten really smart or gone through successful counseling, the script is already written.

We tend to couple with people who play out the same scripts.

➥

When Something Changes Everything

Lost love, we started and ended as strangers.
And now that I've loved
you,
do I have to hate
you
to be able to like
you?
I would like to be able to like you.
I need to believe you're a nice person
with snakes in your brain.
Believing that makes me seem less a fool.

SEE: **THIRD ENERGY, REBOUNDS,
SEXUAL 911**

Peter McGugan

Solitude

Solitude is not your punishment. It is a pause, a reflection. The root of this word is sol—light.

It is when you are quiet with your thoughts that the light can dawn on your consciousness.

To fear this process is to fear your Self and Life.

SEE: **ALONENESS, SUPPORT SYSTEMS**

Soul Recovery
Mending The Broken Heart

We describe loss as "heart shattering." We say, "I gave them my heart," "broken hearted," "a heart rending experience." Rending means to separate into parts with violence, to tear in grief.

Loss shatters the soul.

It is clearly in our language, "I'm out of my mind with grief," "I gave them my heart," "hang onto your heart," "pulling your heart strings," "the best parts of me went with them." What these all express is that we're not fully present in the body—that pieces of consciousness or spirit are absent.

Here are the steps for mending the broken heart. It requires surrender, faith and release. Most of all it requires courage. At the end you will feel more in control of yourself, more healed, more normal.

1. Find a quiet, safe place and relax. Breathing slowly and comfortably, gradually allow a warm and comforting liquid relaxation to dissolve tension from all parts of your body.

2. Become aware of your heart as if you have an inner camera. Sense the appearance or feeling of it. Are there dark or empty places there? Are there dull parts or wedges of energy missing?

Peter McGugan

3. Sense where those missing pieces are. You may follow a silvery thread to find these lost pieces of yourself.

4. This energy belongs within you. Ask for it back. Everyone is better if you recover this lost part of yourself.

5. Affirm that you will only let pure and light filled parts of yourself enter; then receive it and let it melt back into your heart.

This can be an extremely profound and powerful experience for many people. It is also one we may resist because we think lost loves need that piece of us with them. Or we feel lost without them.

If your lost love is only alive in spirit form, sense whether they have gone into The Light and are at peace. Affirm that they must go into The Light to be safe and whole. Realize that your clinging energy is an encumbrance to them.

Sometimes releasing loved ones into The Light has to be negotiated within you and negotiated with them. It is very important for you to release them into The Light.

After doing this, you will feel more at peace; in your chest you may notice a pleasing fullness you haven't had lately.

Parts of your consciousness may have been, as we say, "out of your mind" or "in another world."

➡

When Something Changes Everything

For now you belong in this world.

Mending your broken heart makes you stronger, more centered, happier, funnier, forgiving, more resourceful, creative and healed.

You may want to have a friend read this process to you. This process is also an important part of the "When Something Changes Everything" tape program.

Peter McGugan

Stages Of Grief

Grief is fluid. It's more random than ordered. You feel beyond one phase and you're suddenly back into the previous one.

We do not move cleanly from one into the next, there is no correct order, and some lessons of loss linger much longer than others.

Although it may feel as though you've fallen back into the same old pit, as long as the grieving process is not diluted with drugs or paralyzed by avoidance, there is progress. Retrace the steps you've taken and redo the things that moved you forward.

Shock

Even when a loss is long anticipated, there is shock. Natural numbness often gets us through the funeral or other rituals and then wears off after five or six weeks. The numbness lasts longer if you deny emotions.

SEE: IMPACT, RECOVERY,
GRIEF PRIMER,
FRIENDS

➥

Emotional Release

When the numbness dissipates, intense anger, fear, remorse and loneliness can follow. Fault and blame become preoccupations and even obsessions. The trials of the mind begin. We are often amazed to discover the depth of our love and the breadth of our hopes.

We build great expectations, often subconsciously; when all possibility is gone, these harbored hopes reveal themselves. Feelings of failure and low self-esteem are common here.

SEE: TRIALS IN YOUR MIND, THINKING THINGS THROUGH

Depression

Depression is a cocktail of intensely heavy emotions, blended with feelings of helplessness and hopelessness. There is always anger at the root of depression. Someone or something familiar and cherished is gone and the void feels vast. The yearning to be near them, to be able to go back and relive the past, to do it over again is extremely intense. These are the hollowest days of living. We wonder how and why the world goes on. All fun has gone, and we are often offered artificial mood boosters.

SEE: CHEMICAL DEPENDENCY

Physical Symptoms Of Distress

Experiencing pain in the area where the deceased was most ill or wounded is a way of connecting to their experience. "I feel your pain" is a familiar phrase in our

Peter McGugan

language. Intense empathetic pain is most common among grieving children, who may subconsciously be trying to bargain a dead or dying person back to a healthy life by experiencing their pain.

Anxiety

Fear of distance from a loved one and of someday not being able to recall their smile, face or voice can cause acute anxiety. We are face to face with mortality—theirs, yours, everyone's. Death is frightening, especially for people who've been taught we are the children of a judgmental and punishing God.

If we perceive unexpected death as punishment rather than process or reward, we will be frightened.

Birth and death are not pretty, however they are every soul's natural evolution.

Anger

Random and illogical or targeted, rage is laser pointed at all we perceive to be responsible. Doctors, God, guardian angels, relatives and the deceased are open targets.

The intensity of our rage is often confusing, socially inappropriate and spiked with guilt.

Rage has the same intensity as the human force that empowers a mother to lift a car off her injured child.

Learning to direct rage in healing ways is a vital part of full recovery.

SEE: **ANGER**

➡

When Something Changes Everything

Guilt

Death and loss amplify problems that existed in the relationship, creating seemingly unresolvable obstacles for the survivor. Days and nights of should'a, could'a, would'a can be soothed by rational explanations, but guilt lingers until resolution is achieved.

As a form of self-punishment and an expression of low self-esteem, we find ways to blame ourselves. We selfishly try to own events totally, to put ourselves in the center of every aspect.

Let others own their lives, their choices, their destiny and their deaths.

SEE: GUILT, FORGIVENESS

Fear

Fear is the opposite of Love. When Life shocks us and death carries away someone we love, we can fear death, fear life and fear love. We can fear our own home, fear leaving home, fear being alone and fear new relationships. Each day is treacherous until we find the courage and knowledge to face the monsters that frighten us and make peace with them.

SEE: LOVE OVER FEAR, OBSESSING, NIGHTTIME

Peter McGugan

Surrender

As with any deep wound, there is a tender scar requiring care and healing. With time the wound becomes strong and less sensitive. Stronger, in fact, than the unwounded areas.

Eventually the tenderest aspects of the loss can be touched, examined and accepted, and we are grateful for today.

SEE: SURRENDERING

Peace With It

As mental, physical and spiritual adjustment to the loss settle in, the happy times, echoes of the past can warmly be remembered and cherished with gratitude. We're less angry for what we've lost and thankful for what we had and have.

When the memories bring a smile and feelings of warmth rather than emptiness, anger and longing, the heart is successfully healed.

When Something Changes Everything

Strategies For Achieving

It is helpful to realize people use one strategy to manage change.

The key to people with different achievement styles is to understand their agenda and align the new action plan so it includes feedings for their emotional or material hungers.

Shark Strategies

Raised in a climate of competition and scarcity, the shark believes there isn't enough to go around and they have to do whatever it takes to get theirs' first.

- They're addictive personalities, adrenaline junkies lacking in flexibility compassion and insight.

- Their brain runs on the stressful must-win neurochemicals of fear.

- Sharks influence situations with big performances. They roil the waters creating a flurry of frenzy and uncertainty.

- Because they play a scarcity game sharks believe there is a winner and a loser in every interaction.

- The shark's natural cover is confusion. They lateral issues by bringing up past insignificant weakness, influence the people they've destabilized and glide into the shadows.

Peter McGugan

- Locked into ego, maintaining a perception of control, they aggressively maneuver to get theirs first. When they get yours too, they can direct you through control and fear.

- Motivated by fear themselves, they believe it is the ultimate motivator for everyone.

- To be in control requires constant patrol. Being a shark is exhausting, lonely and takes a long-term toll on health.

Working With A Shark

In a state of ego we are inflexible, we don't listen, learn or adapt. Ego is emotional darkness.

The shark is spiritually and emotionally handicapped, and to accomplish things with them means aligning the result with their agenda.

Know what, why, where, when and how to make your ideas work for them before you go through their door. Have your homework done and be able to support your statements.

And when your plan works, you'd be smart to let the shark think it was all their idea.

The challenge for you is whether you need the result more than you need to own the credit for it.

Turtle Strategy

Gentle and patient listeners, turtles seem to be friendly, thoughtful and harmless. They like to be liked and think being publicly agreeable, polite and pleasant builds popularity.

- Turtles listen to new ideas and may even smile upon discussions of change, but in their hearts they believe our role is to preserve the old order, because that minimizes risk. They privately cite the old book of rules and use history to chart the future.

- The arch enemy of change, a turtle's agenda is *"clinging to safety and security and holding onto what I've got by not risking change."* They think good managing is holding on for dear life.

- Turtles appear to go along with things until the crucial moment. Then they'll introduce facts or opinions that paralyze progress. Loyal to the past, change elicits a nasty snap and turtles become saboteurs.

- When the price of not responding to change has to be paid, turtles use blame, shame and 'nothing could have been done' as excuses, before retreating into their shell.

- If it isn't sunny, safe and warm, turtles hide. They resist getting into the middle of the game, feeling safer manipulating with doubt and fear in the muddy shadows.

- Because turtles have low self-esteem does not mean they have low self-confidence. Don't assume they won't execute their private agenda.

Peter McGugan

A TURTLE IS REPORTING BEING MUGGED
BY A PAIR OF SNAILS.
THE OFFICER ASKS THE TURTLE TO DESCRIBE
THE SNAIL ASSAILANTS.
"I CAN'T," SAYS THE TURTLE "IT ALL HAPPENED SO FAST!"

Working With A Turtle

Turtles get promotions and positions on committees
and boards because they seem pleasant, solid and personable.

To get results with them, get into their shell and
understand their fears. Convince them of the urgency
of the situation long before decisions have to be made
or votes are taken.

Find out what they're afraid of losing if they support
change. Often it is a secondary or selfish issue. Can that
aspect be salvaged for them? Research and then communicate the present and future reality and the consequences of not responding.

Spell out the future if they don't respond to change.
Let them see the doom of not adapting.

To a turtle, the decision to change can feel like a
huge loss, a betrayal of the past and an admittance of
failure. Communicate with and coddle them through
the process.

The Dolphin Strategy

Personable, resourceful and resilient, dolphins read currents, use flow and respond in unison or independently. They play as they thrive in a tough environment.

- Dolphins know scarcity and abundance are possible and take responsibility for what they create. Highly evolved, dolphins disengage from past behavior and ingeniously reinvent the game.

- Dolphin personalities peak as gentle leaders who give self-esteem, opportunity and choice away. They know the source of prolonged influence flows from giving possibility and power to others. Their agenda is to find the win/win/win action and make the implementation work for all.

- Smart and patient, dolphins are deadly to sharks. While a shark may get a taste of dolphin blood, dolphins who save themselves thrive.

Peter McGugan

Working With A Dolphin

Because they are busy people, dolphins want your research and fact finding done so you aren't wasting their time. Support your understanding of the situation with facts and present three possible courses of action.

Present the ways your ideas benefit everyone and together create the most elegant and optimal idea to start developing.

Stay flexible and communicative with the dolphin. Answer questions and support your actions with facts and knowledge verified by voices of experience.

Efficient progress reports will keep the dolphin invested, networking and supporting you.

Conclusion

Everyone always has an agenda built on their values, and the key to working with anyone is matching actions that support their agenda with actions that support yours.

Strength

We either attract a lesson to ourselves because we need to learn it—or we are strong enough to participate in the lessons of others.

Big things happen not for just one reason, but for a thousand reasons. Understanding them is not required here on Schoolhouse Earth.

We cannot really understand WHY until we view life from the vantage of angels.

Be patient with yourself, with Life.

List your sources of strength...and draw from them.

SEE: **WHY, SUPPORT SYSTEMS**

Peter McGugan

Support Systems

EXERCISE

The things that lift and support you are vitally important now. They are natural tonics. Moment to moment we use our supports to prop ourselves up.

Gradually through your support system, you are moving toward happiness.

On the lines below, list all you have to support you. Include friends, pets, walks in the park, creative activities, homemade soup, music, warm baths, hobbies...

My Support System

- _____
- _____
- _____
- _____
- _____
- _____
- _____
- _____
- _____
- _____
- _____

Post this support system on the refrigerator and near your desk, bed and favorite chair. When you feel a hollow need, scan the list. Really ask yourself which support you want now.

Add new activities to the list.

Varying your supports keeps you balanced and fulfilled. You'll not be dependent on just one choice, person or substance.

If your support system is lacking variety expand it now. This is very important.

Life still offers you a wondrous variety of choices. Many of the best—sunsets, parks, galleries, museums, walks, friends—don't require money.

In the past what have you wished you had time for?

Loss offers gains that invite us to begin another chapter.

SEE: **LOSS AND GAINS**

Surrendering

When something has changed everything, some people stubbornly cling to the unraveling past, dangling from its last weak threads.

Angry, feeling cheated, they refuse to surrender because it would require taking responsibility for their future, a future that asks them to recreate themselves.

They deny possibility.

Their resistance cultures pain.

Pain = connection so it serves a masochistic purpose.

This choice is passive suicide. It makes the angels weep.

SEE: RESISTANCE

NOW IS A RAZOR-SHARP MOMENT
CUTTING A BROAD WAKE THROUGH TIME,
FOREVER SEVERING PAST FROM FUTURE.
IT IS DONE.
LET GO
AND LET GOD.

Survival

The fact you have survived to this moment, that you are reading these words, means you still have a contract of purpose with Creation.

Open to that purpose and make it your reason for facing the dawn.

If you cannot find this purpose, your life is too contained. Go beyond yesterday's boundaries and find a hunger you can feed, a person you can comfort, an animal you can save or a cause you can live for.

Life fills the vacuums of loss, when we let Life in.

Peter McGugan

Thinking Things Through

Lying down is a good idea during an earthquake.

Each loss measures on your emotional Richter scale. For each number it registers, there are tears to cry.

Pain does not store well.

As much as you may want to dodge the pain, there is no escape.

You must wonder, wander, ponder and poke through the ashes of your history and dreams.

Probe the "should haves," "could-haves," and "would-haves," the "what-ifs," "if-only-I'ds" and "maybe-ifs" until you are exhausted.

Only when you are convinced there is nothing to salvage can you be finished and leave the scene.

SEE: **DRUGS**

➡

EVERY THOUGHT
PASSES THROUGH YOUR MIND.
THE THOUGHTS YOU ALLOW TO LINGER
DEFINE YOU.

Peter McGugan

Third Energy: The Ocean Of Love

What is born when two lovers connect? That ticklish nectar of the heart is the chemistry, the pool of love, the third energy.

It is the heart's warm Gulf Stream, the ethereal child of Loving.

It transcends the bodies.

This chemical, emotional, magnetic, spiritual flow links lovers no matter the distance between them.

It softens life's edges and buoys us until the focused connection is contaminated or dammed.

And we flounder in the hurricane backwash of our own Love, gasping, choking, drowning in the sucking undertow of a turbulent ocean—the heart's Bermuda Triangle.

Until we cut free, let go and break for the surface.

Alone.

And create our life raft.

Time

Life is an ever changing kaleidoscope.

Without what you've perceived to be destruction, there can be no creation, for energy must end in one form to begin in another.

It is only with the two angels of recovery—Distance and Time—that you can view the creative energy of endings.

Peter McGugan

Time and Reality

On television, catastrophe hits and we go to commercial. We come back and everything is much better already.

HEY...LIFE,
WE'RE WAITING FOR THE COMMERCIALS!

Hollywood condenses Life's most complicated problems into an hour punctuated with commercial breaks. It requires almost 100 people to work a full day to create 2 to 3 minutes of "Hollywood reality." We poor fools, sitting in the dark, believe reality is up there on the screen and our life is not nearly enough.

We are the first generations to have been subjected to thousands of hours of the Hollywood dream, and it has impaired our awareness of Life's truths.

SEE: **THIRD ENERGY, REBOUNDS, SNAKES IN THE BRAIN, SEXUAL 911**

Trials In Your Mind

Recovery can involve a cerebral court battle to understand who did what, why, when, where and how.

The trial drags on, you being prosecutor, defendant, judge, jury and prisoner.

Putting people on trial is natural and necessary when questions need settling.

The verdict: everyone is guilty and everyone is innocent.

Violations of the heart usually result in hung juries.

At some point, the trial in your mind needs to end.

The sentence handed down to ourselves by ourselves is "It is done. I have learned. Let go and let God."

SEE: **VIOLENCE AND REVENGE**

FACED WITH THE CHOICE OF CHANGING ONE'S MIND AND PROVING THAT IT ISN'T NECESSARY, MOST PEOPLE GET BUSY ON THE PROOF.

Peter McGugan

Tribal Customs

Some East Indian tribes give members new names and ways of dressing as they mature through the seasons of their lives. They believe that, in the course of a lifetime, we are five different people, and they support this reinvention process.

It's logical, isn't it?

In many tribal societies following the death rites for a spouse, the widowed one is taken to a solitary place and allowed to empty themselves of the past. Then, when they return to the tribe, they live in a new place.

There is merit in it.

WHEN SOMETHING CHANGES EVERYTHING,
WE NEED TO PLAN FOR WHO WE ARE BECOMING
MORE THAN WHAT WE'VE BEEN.

Tutors

TO BE EXCELLENT AT LIFE,
FIND A CHILD
WILLING TO TUTOR YOU.

We're so good at life when awareness is fresh. Children are instinctively good at being in each moment and not anchoring their feelings to the past or future.

Peter McGugan

Violence And Revenge

Violent acts against people are never, ever a resolution. Violence just shifts and magnifies your problems. It will compound your pain and multiply your foes.

It will make the complicated things you feel now seem light hearted. If you spend time thinking about revenge, talk out the plan to someone. Talking and describing can often move the anger. If hateful revenge thoughts shroud you, find a therapist who will help you channel that energy more productively.

Revenge doesn't end it. It imprisons us to a lifetime with the essence of the one we seek to destroy.

see: **RAGE AND I, ANGER**

War: The Families

The families of the military experience dramatic, traumatic change punctuated moment to moment by the hypnotic, smoothly hysterical coverage of television.

During televised war, parents of soldiers watch the news up to 22 hours a day, totally paralyzed by fear, not knowing where their child is. Hoping for a reference or a glimpse.

Television becomes the electronic umbilical cord, the lone link for parents who cheered their child's teams from the sidelines of every game.

Leaving the television screen feels like abandonment.

Battles break out on the home front because family members respond so differently.

Worry and grief are extremely personal. We can't expect others to match our timing or choices.

Women often feel they carry the full burden of worrying.

For those who cling to macho scripts, grief is a terrifying monster that is barely contained by work, rage, drugs, alcohol or self-abuse.

It is best to find or form a support group with other families.

Videotape the news coverage so you can get rest and fast forward through what doesn't matter.

Match one another where you can, and allow others to create their process.

Peter McGugan

What's Next?　　　EXERCISE

Resistance to change increases when we can't see where we're going. When we don't know where we want to be and have no plan for getting there, we become afraid, tentative, confused, lost and bogged down.

You need destinations, sweet spots in time, to move toward. If these experiences benefit others it will be easier to find a purpose.

Take a pencil and finish the following sentences three different ways.

I would enjoy_____

_____

_____

It would be nice to_____

_____

_____

If I could, I would go and_____

_____

_____

These sentences are your path to what is next.

SEE: **BEGINNING TO BEGIN**

When Something Changes Everything

Why

WE DO NOT FULLY RESOLVE
OUR LIVES
HERE ON SCHOOLHOUSE EARTH.
UNDERSTANDING WHY
IS A GIFT OF DEATH.
WE RECEIVE IT WHEN WE LOOK BACK
FROM THE VANTAGE OF ANGELS.
UNTIL YOU'RE THERE, *BE* WHERE YOU ARE.
LIFE IS FOR LIVING.

Peter McGugan

Workaholics

Work can provide a mental and emotional refuge, but thoughts are things. They stalk like a panther until we turn and face them.

Workaholics are people on the run. Often what they run from is unresolved grief turned rancid.

Eventually they stumble.

Years or decades later the pain and emotions take the weakened runner down. The old festered wounds open and the emotions flood free.

And these emotional fugitives discover they lost decades, perhaps a lifetime.

SEE: **THINKING THINGS THROUGH, DRUGS, IMBALANCE, HEALING**

Zero Zone

We nest, feathering that nest with people and things, beliefs of security and business as usual. In our cozy nests we snuggle and anticipate sweet spots in time.

But the winds of change reach hurricane force. Something changes everything and we are blown out of that nest and plunged into the Zero Zone.

Flattened by the impact, we lie there and either choose passive suicide or we rise and learn to fly again.

We endure a chilly winter of the soul.

Flight comes after the long slow, step-by-step journey through the emotional swamp and the Zero Zone.

How you cross will be at your own pace. Your history of loss, grief scripts, resiliency and forgiveness determine your path and pace. It is a solitary journey in a group setting.

This is a personal and creative journey. You must be patient with yourself and this strange process.

Avoid propping yourself up temporarily with crutches like chemicals or addictions. They offer only temporary numbness.

It is in the most desperate moments of grief that you empty yourself of a past that no longer can be and fill yourself with your Self.

Pain and grief are valid relations in your family of feelings. A Life is not lived without knowing them.

SEE: **IMPACT**

Peter McGugan

Epilogue

N O LIFE THAT KNOWS PASSION
IS WITHOUT LOSS.

T O STAY ANGRY IS THE CHOICE OF A FOOL.
TO CHOOSE PEACE
AND BE OPEN TO WHAT IS NEXT,
TO ANOTHER PURPOSE FOR BEING,
IS THE CHOICE OF A LIFE MASTER.

Resource Guide

The following guide offers starting points. Think of yourself following a path, working your way through a bureaucratic maze that will lead you to a real person with the solution you need.

Accidents

The Salvation Army or **Red Cross** are equipped to offer emergency help. They can also lead you to other resources. Find them in the white business pages of your phone book.

AIDS

Find AIDS services through the white business pages of your phone book. They can direct you to HIV support groups for everyone affected by AIDS. The **National AIDS Hotline** is (800) 458-5231.

Child Death

Compassionate Friends is a national support group with more than 600 local chapters. They offer understanding, support, referrals and publications for grieving parents and siblings. Their address is P.O. 3696, Oak Brook, IL 60522-3696. (708) 990-0010.

Parents of Murdered Children offers support from 100 E. 8th St. Suite B-41, Cincinnati, OH 45202. They can be reached at (513) 721-5683. See Help!

The Pregnancy and Infant Loss, "**SHARE**", national office is in St. Charles, MO and can be reached at (314) 947-6164.

Canadian Foundation For the Study of Infant Death provide family support, current information and research funding for all of North America. (800) END-SIDS (363-7437).

The **Sudden Infant Death Syndrome Alliance** provides counselling, research and family services through (800) 221-7437.

Alive Alone, Inc. helps parents who've lost all their children. They are at 11115 Dull Robinson Rd., Van Wert OH 45891.

Pen Parents, Inc. publishes a newsletter and connects parents who've lost children through similar circumstances.

(702) 826-7332 P.O. 8738, Reno NV 89507-8738.

Children in Grief

Hospice organizations often run programs for grieving children. Nursing associations also run bereavement programs.

Childhood cancer foundations, often called **Candlelighters**, offer families assistance and counselling. The national number is (800) 366-2223, (301) 657-8401.

The **Compassionate Friends** is an international support group for bereaved parents and siblings. They can be reached through (708) 990-0010 or P.O. 3696, Oak Brook, IL 60522-3696

Children Challenged By Sickness

American Academy of Pediatrics offers pamphlets and books on a wide range of topics at (800) 433-9016.

Ronald McDonald Houses provide lodging, support and in some cases travel assistance for the families of children undergoing treatment. If you are travelling for a treatment, they will connect you with houses in other cities.

Hospice organizations often run support programs for families. They are listed in your yellow pages.

Childhood Cancer Foundations, often called Candlelighters, offer families assistance and counselling. The national number is (800) 366-2223, (301) 657-8401.

The Compassionate Friends is an international support group for bereaved parents and siblings. They can be reached through (708) 990-0010 or P.O. 3696, Oak Brook, IL 60522-3696

Dysfunctional Families

Adult Children of Alcoholics (ACOA) or Al-anon offer guidance. Find them in the white pages of your phone book.

For help with domestic violence contact your local police or a hospital. **The National Domestic Violence Hotline** is (800) 799-7233.

Phobias and Panic

Neuro Linguistic Programming (NLP) can be an effective method of overcoming phobias. Look in the white pages of your business directory for full time NLP practitioners or the yellow pages under Training.

Career Change, Loss of a Job

If you are devastated and not ready to work, keep reading and find a support group. Then identify your passion and career of choice. A book titled, *What Color Is Your Parachute* written by Richard Bolles, publisher: Pacific Pipeline, can help you identify this.

Look in the yellow pages under employment consultants, employment agencies or employment contractors. Go to a book store or library to find guides for writing resumés or interviewing.

If you feel an entrepreneurial spark, read *Working From Home* written by Paul & Sarah Edwards. Publisher: Tarcher/Putnam.

Chemical Dependency

Alcoholics Anonymous or **Narcotics Anonymous** meetings can be found in the white pages of your phone book.

Children in Crisis

The counselling department of your school, your local college or university can recommend a specialist that can evaluate your child's challenges. You might also investigate the **Learning Disability Association of America**, 4126 Library Road, Pittsburgh PA. 15234 phone (412) 341-1515. Tutoring can make a great difference. Check the yellow pages under tutoring.

Codependency

Codependents Anonymous, Nar-Anon or **Al-Anon** will show you paths to liberation and offer companions for the journey. Meetings can be found in the white pages of your phone book. Alcoholics Anonymous can also direct you to these groups.

Compulsions and Addictions

Observe a support group like **Overeaters Anonymous, Gamblers Anonymous, Sex & Love Addicts Anonymous, Workaholics Anonymous, Debtors Anonymous...**

Look for these groups in the white pages of your phone book. Any of these programs will refer you to the best one for you. Alcoholics Anonymous can also direct you to these groups.

Conflicts

Most cities have an **Abuse Hotline**. When relationships become troubled, a counsellor can help you make adjustments. Ask friends, your mental health association or a hospital to recommend three counsellors. Choose the one you both prefer.

There are good books and tape programs in your local book store. An arbitrator may help you negotiate a business understanding. Seek or gather people going through similar changes and form a group. Get guidance for the group from a counsellor.

Crime Violation

Contact the **National Organization for Victim Assistance**, 1757 Park Road NW, Washington, DC 20010. phone (800) TRY-NOVA (879-6682) or (202) 232-6682.

Death or Sickness of a Spouse

Hospice organizations offer tremendous assistance when someone is diagnosed as having six months or less to live. Look in the yellow pages of your phone directory.

The **Widowed Persons Service** has more than 200 chapters nationwide. Their address is, 1909 K Street NW., Washington, DC 20049. They can be reached at (202) 434-2260.

American Association of Retired Persons offers assistance at (800) 441-2277.

Recovery programs are available through places of worship and continuing education programs.

Depression

Find your mental health association in the white business pages of your phone book. For other guidance contact the **National Clearinghouse on Family Support and Children's Mental Health** at (800) 628-1696. See Help!

Disasters

The **American Red Cross** is listed in the white pages of your phone book. They provide immediate disaster and housing assistance. **The Salvation Army** is also ready to help.

Domestic Violence see: conflicts

Graduation

Contact the counselling, career development or employment departments at your local school. Look in the yellow pages under employment consultants, employment agencies or employment contractors. If you have an entrepreneurial spark, read *Working From Home* written by Paul & Sarah Edwards. Publisher: Tarcher/Putnam.

HELP!

Most cities have a 24 hour crisis hotline. Find it in the white business pages or through directory assistance. Some cities have a referral system called *First Call For Help*. It will direct you to people and groups with solutions. Look in your phone book's first five white pages. Community service and important numbers can refer you to agencies that can help. **The United Way**, listed in the white pages, can also lead you to solutions.

Illness

National Organization for Rare Disorders offers reports on rare illnesses, a networking program to link people with the same illness and referrals (800) 999-6673.

Internet Help Sites

Also see our web page that follows
Therapists operating online should be verified before any payment or advice is exchanged. Confirm fees, credentials, guidelines, confidentiality and the schedule.

http://www.metanoia.org/imhs—provides a list of online therapy services.

http://www.apa.org—The American Psychological Association directs users to resources for mental health and a "help center" for guidance with a variety of problems.

http://www.cmhc.com/check—an independent service that has verified the credentials of some therapists working online.

When Something Changes Everything

http://www.cybertowers.com/selfhelp—The Psychology Today of cyberspace sponsored by Self-Help
and Psychology magazines. Daily updates, many subject
departments and research abstracts.
   http://mentalhealth.miningco.com—A guide to
mental health resources on the net.

Learning Disability
   Call the Division of Developmental Disabilities
(800) 843-6154.

Murder
   Parents of Murdered Children offers support from
100 E. 8th St. Suite B-41, Cincinnati, OH 45202.
They can be reached at (513) 721-5683.

Rape, Abuse & Incest National Network
   For support and guidance with these issues
call RAINN at (800) 656-4673.

Separation & Divorce
   Parents Without Partners has more than 800 groups
in the U.S. They provide support, information and
social activities. Call (800) 637-7974. The address is
8807 Colesville Road, Silver Springs, MD 20910.

Stalking
   The **Survivors of Stalking** phone number in Florida
is (813) 889-0767.

Peter McGugan's Web Page: www.petermcgugan.com

Consult our web page for something new:

- insights and updates
- more resources and Peter's other books and tapes
- a schedule of Peter's television appearances, speeches and seminars
- seminars at his Palm Springs mountain ridge retreat
- an opportunity to share your thoughts with others
- information on how to book live appearances by Peter McGugan for your employees, association, business or church

About The Author

Peter McGugan is a best-selling author, broadcaster and therapist.

He is one of America's top-rated speakers and trend-tracking consultants. He is also the change management consultant for many corporations, associations and government agencies.

His first best-seller was *Beating Burnout: the survival guide for the '90s.*

From 1991 to 1997, following multiple personal losses, he embarked on a journey through the "Zero Zone" and the result of his study and experiences is *When Something Changes Everything.*

When not travelling he is relaxing and writing at his mountain ridge home in Southern California.

Reader Path: Accidents And Disasters

Reader Path: Accidents And Disasters (continued)

Reader Path: Career Change, Loss Of A Job

Reader Path: Career Change, Loss Of A Job (continued)

Reader Path: Death Of A Spouse

Reader Path: Loss Of A Child (continued)

Reader Path: Loss Of A Parent

Reader Path: Loss Of A Parent (continued)

Reader Path: Management

Reader Path: Separation, Divorce, Loss Of A Love

Reader Path: Separation, Divorce, Loss Of A Love (continued)